THE TRINIDAD CALYPSO

A Study of the Calypso as Oral Literature

Keith Q. Warner

LONDON
HEINEMANN
KINGSTON   PORT OF SPAIN

Heinemann Educational Books Ltd
22 Bedford Square, London WC1B 3HH
PO Box 1028, Kingston, Jamaica
27 Belmont Circular Road, Port of Spain, Trinidad

IBADAN NAIROBI
EDINBURGH MELBOURNE AUCKLAND
SINGAPORE HONG KONG KUALA LUMPUR NEW DELHI

ISBN 0 435 98790 9

Set in United States of America
Printed in Great Britain by
Richard Clay (The Chaucer Press) Ltd,
Bungay, Suffolk

For Berna,
André,
Charlene,
and
Denise.

ACKNOWLEDGEMENTS

It is a pleasure for me to record my gratitude to all those who, in any way, helped in the writing of this book. My thanks, first of all, to the calypsonians for permission to quote from their work as well as for taking time out to answer countless questions, and, secondly, to those who shared material and ideas; in particular, I wish to single out Oswin Rose, whose extensive collection of original calypso records was a key resource, and Gordon Rohlehr, who followed my work throughout and made welcome suggestions. Joy Clarke, Ian Smart, and my wife Berna are also to be thanked for their meticulous proof-reading.

Keith Q. Warner

University of the West Indies,
St. Augustine, Trinidad and Tobago.

Illustration Credits
"SweetBread" comic strips reproduced by permission of M. Calpu and the *Trinidad Express*. Sheet music reproduced by kind permission of Superintendent Anthony Prospect. Photographs of calypsonians on pp. 52 and 53 reproduced by permission of *Trinidad Express* and *Trinidad Guardian*.

This book is dedicated to all calypsonians...
past, present and future.

Long after most of us are forgotten certain
calypsoes will survive as the only reminders
to some later generation of how we lived,
loved, laboured and sinned.

Albert Gomes (1950)

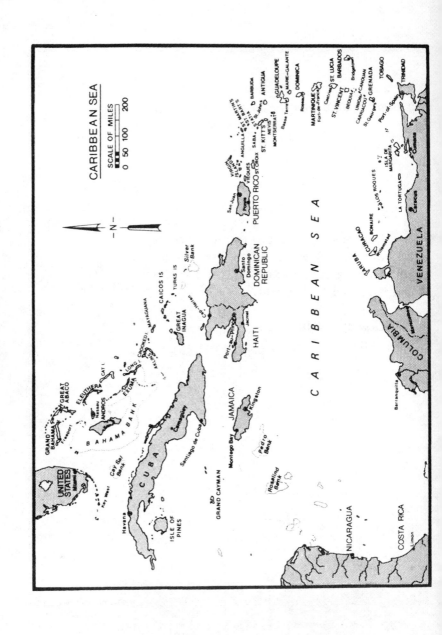

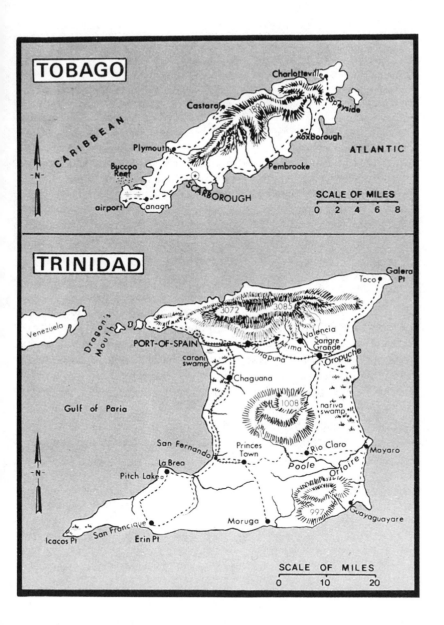

PREFACE

Anyone who has followed my career will know that the road to where I am today was not easy. Come to think of it, it was not only my climb that was difficult but also that of any calypsonian trying to gain for himself and for the profession some measure of dignity and respect. People nowadays keep saying that we have changed calypso over the years. I say why not? We had to change, for Calypso is a live and living thing. The very people complaining about soca and the like would be the first to boo you if you come with the same kind of calypso every year.

The calypsonian, more than anybody else in the society, has to keep his finger on the pulse of the country. His survival depends on knowing what to do to please the public. Yet, some members of that same public are not always one hundred percent behind you, always ready to criticize you when you sing a calypso they don't like, instead of taking time to say a simple 'thank you' for what you've done.

The society as a whole must begin to recognize and appreciate the good in what it has produced—and not only during the Calypso Season! I am proud to be associated with an effort in this direction.

Slinger Francisco
(The Mighty Sparrow)

CONTENTS

ILLUSTRATIONS

INTRODUCTION

Since this book on the contemporary calypso bears the sub-title: "a study of the calypso as oral literature," it is fitting that we clear the air on exactly why we feel that the calypso justifies such a label. The first problem, of course, is deciding on an acceptable interpretation of the term "literature." Wellek and Warren in their *Theory of Literature* see its distinguishing trait as "fictionality," "invention" or "imagination," while admitting that many works are "boundary" cases.[1] To this descriptive conception of literature must be added the evaluative, thus giving a broad definition of literature as creative writings having excellence of form or expression, whatever these latter may be, and as generally in keeping with some widely-accepted norm. The second problem concerns the reluctance with which some accept the fact that literature can be "oral," since the term usually implies a "limitation to written or printed literature," but "clearly, any coherent conception *must include* 'oral literature.'"[2]

When Europeans first went to Africa and failed to find any libraries filled with books, they hastily and erroneously concluded that Africans had no history and no literature. What was overlooked, or deliberately ignored, was the fact that the history and literature had been transmitted orally from generation to generation as part of what has been called the oral tradition. It is this oral tradition which has survived the ravages of time, the Middle Passage and man's inhumanity, and which accounts for the presence in West Indian literature of the unifying elements of so much "folk" material, for it is obvious that, according to Edward Brathwaite, we have to "redefine the term 'literature' to include non-scribal material of the folk/oral tradition, which, on examination, turns out to have a much longer history than our scribal tradition, to have been more relevant to the majority of our people, and to have had unquestionably wider provenance. In other words, while a significant corpus of 'prose' and 'poetry' has been created—and read—by a few persons in the major Antilles; folk song, folk tale, proverb, and chant are found *everywhere* without fear of favor and are enjoyed by all."[3] The calypso is part of this non-scribal material— "literature," considering the conception, "oral," considering the method of transmission.

The vast majority of calypsoes produced yearly are never published in written form (nearly all calypsoes quoted in this book were transcribed from records or tapes) though, increasingly, calypsonians are releasing records of their songs, thus assuring some sort of permanence to their output. In addition, souvenir-type booklets of the more popular calypsoes are also produced, usually by the small private entrepreneur seeking to make a decent profit on his outlay as opposed to the more established publishing houses. The accent is definitely on freshness of composition, if not always of subject matter, and so, except in the case of the "professional" calypsonian, once a calypso serves its purpose for one year, if it is not recorded, it hardly surfaces again in the repertoire of its performer—its purpose being the immediate entertainment or moral upliftment of the listener, or more correctly listeners, since enjoyment of the calypso is, by and large, a communal activity in which both the performer and the audience play well-defined roles. Written publication of these songs is most certainly of secondary, even of minimal importance. "Therefore," wrote Louis James, "when a calypsonian presents us with a piece that in cold print satisfies our intellect as an individual reader, this is an extra bonus, an added excellence to the communal pleasure of performance."[4] This book seeks to provide this extra bonus.

The calypso also owes much of its renown to the usually rhythmic music that accompanies it. Indeed, in many countries the initial recognition of a calypso is by way of its music, a particular rhythm or a particular beat. Ideally, this book should be accompanied by a selection of calypsoes on either record or tape. This would be the easiest way to illustrate how the combination of lyric and melody works, for talking about music—beyond the competence of this author—is very much like talking about food: the ultimate and conclusive test lies in the tasting. Perhaps someone will one day pay due tribute to the Errol Inces, the Bertram Innisses and the John Buddy Williamses, to name but a few, who were so much a part of the many calypsoes on which their music was heard, often turning the calypso with the mediocre lyric into an outstanding contribution by means of very catchy musical arrangements.

Any study of this nature is bound to have restrictions. The main one herein concerns the time covered, namely the period 1956 to 1980. Inevitably, reference has to be made to calypsoes that predate this span, but the starting point in an examination of contemporary Trinidad as a whole can conveniently be set in 1956 because it was in that year that a new political awareness was born with the access to power of the People's National Movement under its leader Dr. Eric Williams, who has managed to retain uninterrupted control of both party and country up to the present time (1980). 1956 is also a convenient starting point for the contemporary calypso, for it was in that year that the Mighty Sparrow sprang into prominence, literally revolutionizing the art form, and he too has retained his position up to the present time.

The second restriction is in the choice of calypsoes and calypsonians. In this regard, what calypsoes were used as illustrations, and from which calypsonians, was largely a matter of personal and arbitrary selection, depending mostly on availability and popularity of the material, since it was pointless relying too heavily on the obscure or the unfamiliar in a work that deals with the calypsonian as the people's entertainer and spokesman.

No apology is made for making such extensive use of the Mighty Sparrow's works, and this for three reasons. First of all, from his initial triumph in 1956, Sparrow has dominated the calypso world, becoming a legend in his own time. As early as 1959, C.L.R. James, in a lecture delivered to the University College of the West Indies on "The Artist in the Caribbean," went as far as to say: "When our local artists can evoke the popular response of a Sparrow, the artist in the Caribbean will have arrived." True enough, he has had his off years, but all in all he has been synonymous with calypso in Trinidad for all this time and, to quote critic Gordon Rohlehr, has "done several different things better than most of his rivals can do the thing in which they specialize."[5] Secondly, Sparrow has for years done more to promote Trinidad culturally on the international stage than many official government missions, and in many countries, even non-anglophone ones, as this author can attest, the information that one was from Trinidad was very often greeted with a smile and the immediate association with a couple of words: "Calypso!...Sparrow!" Consequently, any study of the contemporary calypso that seeks an audience, however limited, outside of Trinidad, must necessarily give pride of place to the Mighty Sparrow. Thirdly, Sparrow's work over the years has been by far more readily available than that of the other calypsonians. Indeed, his LP's were routinely shipped off as gifts to the many friends and relatives residing abroad and many of the latter can still recall the excitement caused by the arrival of each new Sparrow LP. For all this emphasis on Sparrow, however, let it not be said that his rivals did not make an equally important, if not equally voluminous, contribution to the art and as such they too will find themselves featured whenever their work, as opposed to Sparrow's, is the best illustration of the particular point being made.

The final restriction is in the term "Trinidad." The official name of the country is Trinidad and Tobago and much of what is said about Trinidad naturally applies to Tobago. But the majority of calypsonians reside and work in Trinidad, and deal with situations from a Trinidad perspective, hence the "Trinidad" calypso.

The initial reaction of many to the fact that a book was being written on the calypso was one of surprise. The implication was clearly that there is little to write about these popular ditties or about their composers, those happy-go-lucky characters who surface once a year during the calypso season only to return to oblivion during the rest of the year. While this gross generalization, much to the chagrin of many calypsonians, contains an element of truth, as most generalizations do, this book seeks to give the calypso and the calypsonian, at what could be called the level of serious popularization, the critical attention they deserve, an attention that has been, for the most part, long overdue, save, of course, for Gordon Rohlehr's pioneering and penetrating efforts which have been published in various journals or broadcast on radio, and the many academic theses which have so far remained unpublished. A brief history of the evolution of the calypso lays the groundwork for the further examination of what motivates the calypsonians as well as of what goes into their songs and the broader categories into which they fall: commentary on the social and political issues that concern the society; sexually-oriented episodes in which the male calypsonians generally create or maintain their macho image at the expense of the female; or simple anecdotes that are full of humour or fantasy. Finally, following this examination of the calypsonian as artist and the calypso as art form, the image of these two in the written literature of the country that has produced them is itself examined.

NOTES

[1] René Wellek and Austin Warren, *Theory of Literature* (Harmondsworth: Penguin Books, 1963), p. 26.

[2] Ibid., p. 22. My emphasis.

[3] Edward Brathwaite, "The African Presence in Caribbean Literature," *Daedalus,* Vol. 103, No. 2 (Spring 1974), p. 78.

[4] Louis James (ed.), *The Islands in Between* (London: O.U.P., 1968), p. 14.

[5] Gordon Rohlehr, "Sparrow as Poet," in Anthony & Carr (eds.), *David Frost introduces Trinidad and Tobago* (London: André Deutsch, 1975), p. 98.

1

THE EVOLUTION OF THE CALYPSO

Had the aim of this book been to write a history of the calypso from its relatively obscure beginnings through to the present time, what follows in this initial chapter would undoubtedly have taken up the entire volume, so extensive is the field of study. However, since the main thrust lies elsewhere, namely in the appreciation of the calypso in its contemporary form and concomitant function, the details of this history are left to those whose purpose it is to elucidate same. Consequently, the information given on the evolution of the calypso is of a general nature, though, hopefully, adequate enough to enable a full understanding of the subsequent chapters.

Origin of the term "calypso"

The term "calypso" came after the fact of calypso and seems to be either an attempt at refinement or a corruption on the part of the population, struggling at the turn of the century with a fading French patois, in which the majority of the early songs were sung, and an emerging dominance of English. A term that was unfamiliar to new users of English was simply "anglicized" into one that was.

There are in fact several theories on, and great controversy over, the origin of the word. Reviewed here are the main ones put forward over the years, since my own research has not turned up anything that is new.

Nobody seriously contends that it has anything to do with the Calypso of Greek mythology, though one commentator, after reviewing the various possible origins and conceding that "the name Calypso is a misnomer and bears no direct relation whatever to the folk music of Trinidad itself," does venture to add: ". . . it is still not certain that the English or Americans on coming to Trinidad and hearing the expression used for the folk music and feeling its enchanting effects did not misinterpret the word to mean 'Calypso' of Greek mythology."[1]

Akin to this bit of speculation is another equally ingenious and amusing one by Helen Russell: ". . . a resident here. . . recalls the arrival in the island in past days from Curacao of a lady singer of easy virtue named Calypso (creole: calyso) but more commonly known as Bim-Bim. Her songs were pronouncedly risqué; neither she nor they were mentioned in polite society. It seems probable that the lady's songs were called by her name, and, by the association of ideas, the name became adopted for carnival improvisations..."[2] One thing is certain: no serious student of the calypso will entertain the thought that it could have come, either in name or in form, from Curacao.

The transformation into "calypso" is seen to have come from one of these sources:
a) the Carib word "carieto," meaning a joyous song, which itself evolved into "cariso;"
b) the French patois creations "carrousseaux" from the archaic French word "carrousse," meaning a drinking party or festivity, or "caillisseaux," an apparent attempt to give a French form to a term transmitted orally, probably "kaiso," of which this form would be an acceptable rendition in writing;
c) the Spanish word "caliso," a term also used for a topical song in St. Lucia;
d) "careso," a topical song from the Virgin Islands;
e) the West African (Hausa) term "kaiso," itself a corruption of "kaito," an expression of approval and encouragement similar to "bravo."
This is the derivation that has found the most favour. Hence we find Raymond Quevedo, the knowledgeable calypsonian of the early half of this century, claiming that "kaiso" was the first term he knew, though it evolved into "calypso" via "caliso," "rouso" and "wouso."[3]

This last term "kaiso" has also survived alongside its derivation "calypso," which, according to Errol Hill, first appeared as "calypso," denoting the Trinidad Carnival song only in 1900.[4] It is still used to show appreciation for a calypso well composed and executed. Thus Quevedo's statement about "kaiso" being used to describe the song when sung as well as a means of expressing ecstatic satisfaction over what was in the opinion of the audience a particularly excellent "kaiso" is still valid today, a state of affairs that does not seem to be in any way on the decline.

The dual existence of an original word alongside its etymological derivative is nothing new. The difference in them is usually one of pure semantics. Hence "kaiso," in addition to its main role as indicator of appreciation and approval, is at times also used interchangeably for "calypso." In such a case it has the connotation of "genuine calypso." In recent times, there has been in some circles a favouring of the term "kaisonian" to designate one who sings "genuine" calypsoes, as opposed to "calypsonian" for the run-of-the-mill. Be that as it may, the term "calypso" seems well entrenched.[5]

The first calypsonians
Opinion is also equally divided on who were the first calypsonians, particularly since, as we have seen, what was being sung only came to be called calypso much later on. Among well-informed commentators there appears

to be some measure of agreement with information supplied by Mitto Sampson to the effect that what eventually evolved into the contemporary calypso started at the time of French settlement in Trinidad in the late eighteenth century. The first chantwell[6] or singer of cariso was Gros Jean, appointed "Maît' Caiso" (Master of Kaiso) to a certain Pierre Begorrat, who had come from Martinique in 1784 and had settled down to a rather royal-like existence, complete with the holding of court in a cave on his property. "The court was attended by African slave singers of 'cariso' or 'caiso,' which were usually sung extemporare and were of a flattering nature, or satirical or directed against unpopular neighbours or members of the plantation community, or else they were 'mépris,' a term given to a war of insults between two or more expert singers."[7]

Three points need to be made immediately. From the very beginning some of the elements that were later to become the hallmark of the calypso were present in the songs. First of all, they were usually sung extempore. To this day, when nearly all calypsoes are composed and rehearsed before rendition, the ability of the calypsonian to sing extempore is greatly admired and appreciated. Secondly, they were flattering or satirical, foreshadowing in this respect the many biting social comments that inform the contemporary calypso. Thirdly, the singers would trade insults among themselves, thus starting the tradition of what were to become the celebrated calypso wars. In this regard, therefore, the slaves who practised this "art" can definitely rank among the forerunners of the contemporary calypsonian. It is to be noted, *en passant,* that they were not entirely without a tradition of their own in the area of songs of praise and derision, having, to all appearances, brought this with them from West Africa.[8]

The post-Emancipation period in Trinidad saw other singers continuing the tradition established by names such as Soso, Papa Cochon, Lord Hannibal and Surisima, a Carib Indian who claimed that these "carisos" were Carib in origin.[9] Around this time the native songs were also called "belairs" (sometimes "bélés"), seen by some commentators as the direct forerunner of the modern calypso. But this first generation of singers, as it were, was followed by a second that owed its existence to two main factors: the demographic pattern following Emancipation and the development of Carnival. For some commentators, it is this second generation of chantwells that constituted the earliest calypsonians.[10]

Calypso and Carnival

By the 1970's the Trinidad Carnival had become so well-known throughout the island, the Caribbean and the world that hotel and travel reservations for those wishing to visit Trinidad to see it had to be made several months in advance. Little did many of the revelers realize that, a century or so before, the official government backing and general approval with which present-day Carnival is viewed were almost non-existent, and

the very thought that the government was planning to stop Carnival had led
to rioting in 1881.

Pre-Emancipation Carnival was celebrated by the white Creole upper
class with masked balls, house to house visiting, street promenading and
not-too-harmful practical jokes.[11] Post-Emancipation Carnival changed
this picture drastically as the "freed Africans celebrated it with songs, street
dancing and stick-fighting, which often became open rioting. Scores were
evened at Carnival time, houses stoned or burnt, and scathing criticisms
levelled at the powerful by the powerless."[12]

Historian Bridget Brereton writes:

Around the 1860's Carnival came to have a distinctive
character: the 'Jamet' Carnival of the *diamètre* class.[13] The
festival was almost entirely taken over by the jamets, who
had created in the backyards of Port of Spain their own
sub-culture. Here the urban lower class lived in long bar-
rack ranges situated behind the city blocks, centering on a
yard which formed a common living space. At about this
time, yard 'hands' were formed: groups of men and
women, boys and girls, who went around together for singing, fighting and dancing. Such bands existed all the year
round, *but were especially active in the weeks before Carnival, when they rehearsed their songs, dances and stick-
fighting. The yard 'chantwelle,' or singer, insulted rival
yards* and yard stickmen sought out rivals for single com-
bats.[14]

The demographic push into certain areas of Port of Spain by the freed
slaves was largely responsible for the creation of a sub-culture. Carnival
provided one sure outlet for their stifled creative energies, particularly for
the leaders of the newly-formed bands. "Each band had its lead singer, or
chantuel...whose task was to harangue the stick-fighters into action, to
sustain the courage of his champion, and to pour scorn on the rival group
and champion. Each lead singer was supported by a chorus drawn from
among the band." So writes Gordon Rohlehr after concluding that "these
were the earliest calypsonians."[15]

Carnival survived and moved into the twentieth century and the chantwell evolved into the calypsonian. "In the street masquerades, the calypsonian was attired to represent one of the principal characters in the band, second only to the king. In this costume, he would render his songs and take
on qualities of the character he portrayed...The whole company was knit
together by the calypso songs."[16] The Carnival/Calypso association remained, grew tighter in fact, to the point where calypsoes were recognized
in relation to the carnival season of a particular year. Increasingly, new
calypsoes were geared to presentation during the pre-Carnival season. They
lost some of the spontaneity of the chantwell leading the band and became

well-prepared and well-rehearsed numbers to be presented to the public during the "calypso season." Many calypsonians surface only during this season, stretching from the start of the New Year through to Carnival, and are not heard from again until the beginning of the following season.

The Carnival/Calypso association is further strengthened by the fact that virtually all the music played by the Carnival bands comes from the new calypsoes, with the result that, in the mind of the Trinidad public, every new Carnival means a new crop of calypsoes. This unwritten law is so strict that in recent times, with the advent of high-pressure sales techniques to push newly-cut calypso records, calypsonians who have released their records very early in the season, even in late November or December, run the risk of not finding favour with the "tent" audiences for "coming with an old song." Despite efforts to keep calypso alive throughout the year, Carnival and calypso remain closely-knit cultural twins.

The Calypso Tents

It was an established practice in the weeks preceding Carnival "for masquerade bands to assemble at night in backyard tents and rehearse their calypso choruses... Now at last people of influence began to attend the tent practices to get a foretaste of the new songs and to enjoy an evening of native wit and spicy humour."[17] What was true of the pre-World War I tents has remained unchanged up to the present time: the preview of coming songs as well as the wit and spicy humour.

Following World War I, the practice tents—and they were indeed tents—were drawing so many followers that a small fee was charged for admission. "As yet," says Errol Hill, "there is no mention of a stage platform. Calypsonians sang from the floor of the tent, almost totally surrounded by the audience, which was seated on rough bamboo benches or which lounged around the sides of the enclosure."[18] One result of this formalization of presentation was the toning down, but not total disappearance, of the extempore nature of the calypso in favour of carefully rehearsed renditions.

The modern tent is said to be the brainchild of one Walter Douglas, a World War I veteran, who is said to have opened his first tent in 1921. There is a claim by calypsonian Houdini that it was in fact he who erected the first tent in 1920—The Chinese Junk Yard[19]—and Gordon Rohlehr states that Norman LeBlanc (Richard the Lion Heart) "opened the first calypso 'tent' and was charging a small fee by 1903."[20] Douglas is credited with various innovations: the use of tarpaulin to cover the bamboo structure, the use of gas lamps instead of kerosine flambeaux, the replacement of the bamboo benches with rented chairs, the printing of tickets to advertise his shows, the use of guest calypsonians and the erection of an open platform stage for singers and orchestra.[21] These represented quite an achievement for the period and foreshadowed the modern tent in more ways than one.

Use of the term "tent" has persisted over the years even though calypsoes are no longer presented in a real tent. A variety of halls, cinemas and
other accessible buildings have served as calypso tents. Early tents actually
had to shift locality from "vagabond areas" to avoid problems with the
"hooligan" element and to create and maintain an air of social respectability.[22] In addition, the 1930's saw a period of police censorship, with calypsoes being banned for being profane.

In recent times, a tent has had a "lead" or "main" calypsonian by
whose name the tent is familiarly known. For example, the Original Young
Brigade was for many years known as Sparrow's tent and the Calypso
Revue as Kitchener's. There has been much "tent hopping" by calypsonians in search of better conditions and this has at times led to confusion at
the start of the calypso season over "who singing where." One most
welcome development has been the taking of the "tents" to the other towns
and to the University Campus, thus lessening the Port of Spain stranglehold
as the centre of calypso.

Innovations have naturally been perfected to the point where the public
has come to expect certain amenities at the tents, including an excellent
sound reproduction system to capture the calypsonian's every sigh and
grunt as clearly as possible. Whereas the earlier tents allowed the audience
to see only the upper half of the calypsonian, in recent times the latter has
been appearing on stage alone and in full view of the audience, a much more
"vulnerable" situation, to say the least.

The tent is atmosphere; and the atmosphere is one of *laissez-aller* and
"fatigue" or heckling. The more popular tents attract so many patrons and
the latter are forced to be in their seats so early that the audience as a whole
is looking for the slightest pretext to let off steam, either in its enthusiastic
approval of a number or in its vociferous rejection of a mediocre performance. The contemporary audience is comprised of a blend of all classes
and races, though in the late 1940's and early 1950's the clientele, according
to both Lord Pretender and Lord Superior, was mostly white.

Invariably, almost characteristically, the show begins late, usually after
a few slow hand-claps from the impatient audience. Once on stage, the
calypsonian uses either the microphone hand-held, allowing himself greater
mobility, or stands in one spot singing into the microphone set on a stand.
The choice is largely one of personal style, though some calypsonians do use
both methods. Now that he is no longer seen only from the waist up, greater
attention is paid to dress. In the early life of the tents, calypsonians appeared in "jacket and tie," no doubt to lend an air of respectability to their
craft. Many are the stories of one jacket making the rounds from calypsonian to calypsonian, since not every one could afford to buy his own.
Calypsonians evolved their own brand of dress—a mixture of the latest
styles plus some personalized touch—and as a result a gaudily dressed individual would be said to be "looking like a calypsonian." The recent trend

has been to have special "show" outfits, particularly if the singers also perform in nightclubs, and to dress for the part, to wear a costume depicting the topic of the calypso. The Mighty Sparrow, for example, has appeared as a schoolchild in uniform, as a college professor in academic robe, as King Kong and as a robot...Numerous others appear as a motley assortment of characters. The calypsonian has also had to become a "showman."

The crucial link between audience and calypsonian is the Master of Ceremonies, the M.C. Himself one of the calypsonians, he not only introduces the singers, but puts the audience in the proper frame of mind with a blend of verbal acrobatics, jokes and heckling. The tent audience, having come to hear the risqué songs that are not aired on the radio and which may not always be available on record, expects some degree of spicy patter from the M.C. and the jokes given between numbers must keep the tone. Followers of the calypso recognize Lord Melody as the dean of M.C.'s, a role he hardly assumes any more, but by far the best in the 1970's is Bill Trotman, the M.C. at the Original Young Brigade, where he shares this role with Tobago Crusoe. Trotman, who sings calypsoes as Trinidad Bill, has a history of comic routine rather than calypso singing. His timing and delivery of jokes are excellent and any "fatigue" from the audience is immediately met with a biting rejoinder. Trotman as M.C. is always master. The contemporary M.C., therefore, must be quite skilled in "picong," continuing the practice where even the calypsonians have all but abandoned it.

As we have seen, shouts of "kaiso" punctuate the well-liked performance. In addition, prolonged applause after the calypsonian has left the stage is a signal for the orchestra to break once more into the bars of the song just rendered and for the calypsonian to return for an encore. This can go on for three or more stanzas. What really goes down well is for the calypsonian to have a new stanza ready for each encore or for him to compose one extempore if none is ready. More often than not, though, the calypsonian merely repeats one of the stanzas already sung. On the negative side, disapproval of a calypso is met with either slow hand-clapping while the calpsonian is still performing or with loud jeers and shouts that leave no doubt about the audience's displeasure. Nor is previous success, even during the same night, any guarantee of sympathetic response from the audience. Many a calypsonian has received two or three encores for his first number, only to return to a barrage of catcalls and boos in the presentation of his second. In this regard, the tent audience is ruthless and gives no quarter.

Picong

As in so many other instances in the semantic history of English as spoken in Trinidad, a French patois word provided the origin of a term in the Trinidadian's vocabulary. The term "picong" is derived from the French "piquant" (stinging, insulting) and referred originally to the caustic insults that were traded during the exchanges by rival chantwells in the early days. The tradition of verbal insults was continued well into the development of the tents and evolved into the "calypso war," with inter-tent rivalry. Errol Hill provides a good account of what happened during one of these wars: "a competitor in these duels usually rendered his complete composition at one go, which was followed by a suitable rebuttal in his opponent's song...The improvisational origin of the calypso was thus perpetuated in the calypso war. Singers lined up at the front stage facing the audience; the orchestra struck up a chorus taken from the theme song of the tent...And the war was on."[23] A veteran of this era, Lord Beginner recalls: "A tent was divided into house, pit and balcony just like the cinema. There were about six calypsonians in a tent. We used to sing many songs in a night. Then at the end, we had 'war,' a battle of words, when all the calypsonians would come on stage and give each other 'fatigue.' That was really great."[24]

Spontaneous improvisation was thus of capital importance, the way it had been at the very beginning. However, there was a limit to what one could improvise under certain conditions while still retaining interest. "Eventually the strain of improvising nightly, after two or two and one half hours of singing rehearsed calypsoes, proved too great for the calypsonians. They began to use stock rhymes and phrases, their verses became highly personal and offensive, or merely banal, lacking sparkle and style. The audiences...started to move out of the crowded tents during the singing of the 'war,' and the practice fell into disuse in the 1950's."[25] The 1970's saw a revival of the tent clashes with, for example, Sparrow's Original Young Brigade pitted against Kitchener's Calypso Revue at shows billed as "The Clash of the Giants," but no calypso war took place at such shows, the performances serving only to give eager audiences the opportunity to see two tents in one night on one stage.

Picong has gradually moved from the calypsonians among themselves and has been replaced by a similar exchange, continued throughout the length of the show, between M.C. and audience, though in a considerably milder tone. The picong war found itself relegated to odd occasions when the "old timers" meet to show the young calypsonians and latter-day audiences how it was done in the old days. Calypsonians still poke fun at one another, however, and the most celebrated case in recent times has been the Mighty Sparrow/Lord Melody duel that was fought via recorded calypsoes in a sort of extra-tent picong. Among the insults traded, Lord Melody called Sparrow "the son of a catarrh-nose Grenadian," accused him of carrying a gun and called his wife "Belmont Jackass." Sparrow retorted that Melody was a smart, conniving pickpocket, called him "ugly and mauvais' langue," accused him of fathering a calf and labelled his wife "Madame Dracula." The words sounded harsh and provocative but were all part of the picong tradition, so everybody loved the interchange, for picong has become part and parcel of Trinidad society, a good-natured though mordant heckling meant to provoke an equally biting response.

Calypsonians and sobriquets

Very few calypsonians sing under their real names. In fact, except for the most popular calypsonians (nearly everybody recognizes Slinger Francisco as the Mighty Sparrow), the real names would go unnoticed if they appeared out of the calypso context, and even in it! The calypsonians retain their official names for their normal non-calypso existence, but, once in the calypso arena, are known to all and sundry by their chosen sobriquet.

Errol Hill gives the following explanation of the start of the practice:

> ...with the upgrading of carnival in the 1890's shant-
> wells of the period were more literate than their
> predecessors. Several from middle-class homes had attend-
> ed secondary school. They had studied European history
> and felt very patriotic toward the "mother country." Bri-
> tain... was then involved in the difficult Boer War against
> "foreigners," and the songsters felt impelled to support
> the home side. They adopted names of the famous war-
> riors, for instance Richard Coeur de Léon, the Duke of
> Wellington, or other combative titles, such as Lord Ex-
> ecutor and King Pharaoh.[26]

The logical extension of this, if we accept Hill's explanation, is to see the budding calypsonians choosing their various *noms-de-guerre* because they too were engaged in their own wars. Hence, Atilla the Hun,[27] the Roaring Lion, who went as far as to change his real name from Hubert Raphael Charles to Raphael de Leon, Lord Kitchener, the Mighty Terror, the Mighty Destroyer, the Mighty Spitfire... This does not explain the names cited by Mitto Sampson.[28] It is not clear whether Lord Hannibal, Papa Cochon or Bodicea were adopted sobriquets or just popular nicknames.

The naming tradition soon settled down to its own set of rules. The sobriquet was a show of grandeur, was meant to inspire confidence, even fear, and so was prefaced either by "the Mighty" or "Lord" or "King." Hence, the Mighty Spoiler, Lord Melody, the Mighty Cypher, King Radio, King Fighter... The Roaring Lion maintains that many young calypsonians arrived at the tents without a sobriquet and were promptly given one by the older calypsonians depending on what was most striking or characteristic about the newcomer.[29] Lord Beginner claims that this was how he received his sobriquet. Admirers were impressed by the prowess of the 15-year-old "beginner" and duly dubbed him such.[30]

Names once used are almost never changed or duplicated, except where a newcomer labels himself as the "Young" version of an established calypsonian. Hence, Young Killer, Young Kitchener... Animals (and birds) and names indicating doers of actions are particularly favoured. Hence, the

Mighty Viper, the Mighty Zebra, the Mighty Cobra, and the Mighty Wrangler, the Mighty Explainer, the Mighty Poser, as well as Lord plus anything: Lord Funny, Lord Almanac... Names of the famous persist. Hence, Lord Eisenhower, King Solomon, Lord Brynner (who actually shaved his head to complete the transformation), the Mighty Stalin (who eventually came to be known as Black Stalin after the M.C. introduced him as such one night)...

With sobriquets having run the gamut of what became stock items, calypsonians increasingly used imaginative names. Hence, Little Mystery, Small Island Pride... Schoolteacher Hollis Liverpool labelled himself the Mighty Chalkdust; one of the tallest calypsonians called himself Lord Shorty; Kelvin Pope chose to be known as the Mighty Duke (and ended up Calypso King!)... Then came Brother Mudada, Sugar Stick, who was to change his sobriquet to Lutha because he did not like the image projected by the former name when he changed his brand of calypsoes, the Merchant and Crazy, always playing the part to the hilt; and some of the established names have been shortened by the calypso aficionados into familiar handles. Hence, Lord Kitchener, who dropped the "Lord" when his country attained Republican status, is known as Kitch, the Mighty Sparrow as just Sparrow or Birdie, the Mighty Chalkdust as Chalkie, Lord Melody as Melo etc. Finally, the trend in recent times has been to drop the "Mighty" and the "Lord."

The female Calypsonian

Legend has it that women sang calypsoes, or carisos, since the nineteenth century. Errol Hill claims that according to "old veterans of the late-nineteenth century carnival...cariso was both a woman's song and a dance."[31] Earlier, Mitto Sampson had spoken of Bodicea, a black female chantwell who loved singing, fighting and drinking, as well as of a Cariso Jane, though he does not actually state that she was a singer.[32] There is also mention of another female chantwell in the late nineteenth century called Big Body Ada. Atilla the Hun is said to have composed a calypso called "A History of Calypso" in which he claimed that women had sung calypsoes "long ago."[33] Journalist Elma Reyes writes of Atilla being "around and active when there was only one woman calypsonian in Trinidad and Tobago."[34] That woman was Lady Iere, who "sang alone and sometimes with her husband Lord Iere... During the Second World War calypso fans hummed Lady Iere's tuneful ditty 'Ice Cream Block'... [in] her heyday in the 50's Lady Iere dominated the airwaves with 'Love Me or Leave Me.'"[35]

Reyes also mentions another female calypsonian from the period of the Second World War. "In the United States during the 2nd World War, a Trinidadian woman, resident in New York, was popular singing as Lady Thelma. She even produced a best-selling commentary of President Roosevelt's decision to approve nightly blackouts. Her calypso was called 'You Gotta Have Power.'"[36]

Apart from these two women (there is also mention of a Lady Beginner) who would have been singing at about the same time, very few took up the challenge until the 1960's with the appearance of Calypso Rose. The reason for this is perhaps best summed up by Gordon Rohlehr. Calypso, he states, "has always been a male mode, whose themes are manhood and the identity of the individual within the group."[37] Of course, this is not all that the calypso is about and as such there seems to be no other real obstacle to the female calypsonian bringing her point of view into the picture. Still, it must have taken great courage to vie with the male calypsonians, especially since the majority of the utterances in calypso were so disparaging to the female on the whole.

Other female calypsonians gradually joined Calypso Rose and the situation has now progressed to the point where there is a Calypso Queen chosen annually. Rose must take some of the credit for this improvement, since she competed with the best of the males and beat them convincingly. Her success over the years—she has been both Calypso Monarch and Road March Queen—cannot but serve as inspiration and incentive for young women who feel their artistic calling lies in the world of the calypso.

On the matter of the sobriquet, female calypsonians merely converted the "Lord" to "Lady" and subsequently continued to use names that identified them as female. Hence, Calypso Princess, Singing Francine, Singing Diane (both of whom added "Singing" to their real first names), Princess B... It is noteworthy that none of the females chose belligerent-type sobriquets, nor have they used the epithet "Mighty."

Calypso competitions

According to Errol Hill, the first known calypso competition was in 1914. It was arranged on Carnival day "by an enterprising business man as an advertising stunt." Subsequently, from 1919 "calypsoes sung by masquerade bands became a standing event at formally organized carnival competitions."[38] That the early competitions centred on the advertising of products is corroborated by calypsonian the Mighty Unknown, who remembers his first competition in 1929 when calypsoes were sung to extol the virtues of Gold Bond Soap. Lord Executor, he recalls, won most of the early competitions.[39]

Lord Beginner also recalls the competitions of the 1920-1930 period: "People were prejudiced to go in the tent, but they filled the theatres and so we use to have big competitions at the Palace and New Theatres in San Fernando, especially when North and South matches were arranged."[40] Competitions were held island-wide and judges were often outstanding members of the budding middle class. Beginner further recalls a competition in 1927 in which he was up against Atilla. He won, at first, but later saw the first prize given to Atilla. The reason given was that Beginner had used a word in his calypso that was not English but patois.[41]

Lord Iere, another veteran of the calypso arena, claims that the idea of a calypso king came from Atilla, who used to crown a king in his tent on the Saturday or Sunday preceding each Carnival. Iere also recalls that the Growling Tiger won the first National King Competition in 1939.[42]

It is therefore not surprising to see the Calypso King Competition incorporated into the privately-run Carnival Queen Show in 1953 and retained in the official Carnival Development Committee's Dimanche Gras Show from 1958. Calypso was at last "officially" recognized. This development really sealed the Calypso/Carnival bond. For many fans who had followed the calypsonians throughout the calypso season, Carnival Sunday Night's Dimanche Gras Show meant the opportunity to find out who the real champion was, though this was not always a clear-cut case. In 1957, for example, the Mighty Sparrow and his colleagues from the Young Brigade staged their own Calypso King Contest in opposition to the "official" competition at the Savannah. Quite appropriately, Sparrow won with "Carnival Boycott," while Lord Pretender won the Savannah competition with "Que Sera, Sera." For calypsonians, being King was a singular achievement and honour, though in later years bitter controversy was to gnaw at the very heart of the entire process.

Several problems almost naturally attend any competition. The Dimanche Gras Calypso King Competition did not escape its share. First of all, the choice of calypsonians to sing at the final. No successful formula has ever been worked out to the satisfaction of all concerned. The latest procedure is to have a panel of judges visit the tents during the calypso season, selecting some two dozen semi-finalists who meet in competition one week prior to the big night. Everyone eagerly awaits the announcement of the seven or eight finalists chosen to vie against the reigning king. Naturally, there are accusations of all sorts levelled at the judges.

Secondly, the criteria used to judge the calypsonians. How many points for originality? Lyrics? Melody? Presentation?[43] Judges and calypsonians never seem to agree on the right blend or ratio within these categories. As a result, several calypsonians have sharply criticized the judges in an almost unending litany and the Carnival Development Committee has been forced to hold pre-Competition seminars to try and sort out the problems.

Thirdly, for those who make it to the final, there is the problem of what to sing, especially if the finalist has a particularly varied repertoire in any one year. In 1961, for example, the Mighty Sparrow, with a variety of songs under his belt, chose to sing "Rose" as one of his selections, only to learn that this was not considered a true calypso. It is generally felt, by calypsonian and public alike, that, for the two calypsoes allowed, a serious-type song of social commentary plus another in lighter vein place the finalist in a very good position. In fact, the Mighty Duke used this formula to win the Calypso King Competition for four consecutive years, a feat unparalleled in recent calypso history. The result of all this is that many calypsonians seek to have in store a "Savannah" tune, guaranteed to take them to the

Queen's Park Savannah where the Dimanche Gras Show is held. Experience seems to indicate that the catchy, peppy calypso, which more often than not has some very stereotyped lyrics about Carnival festivity and which is more suited to the Road March, does the calypsonian little good at the Calypso King Competition. Luckily, there is no hard and fast rule. Even the Mighty Chalkdust, having made the finals for some five years without copping the crown and having sung about the formula he thought to be the winning one:

> If you want to win the crown
> Sing about wine, women and song
> Sing about your neighbour's wife
> Sing about your own sex life

went on to be Calypso King with precisely the opposite of what he advocated, since he stuck to his politically-oriented calypsoes.

With the inclusion of female calypsonians in the competition, one could no longer speak of choosing a Calypso King. As a result, the competition is now billed as one to choose the Calypso Monarch. The Carnival Development Committee also holds a Junior Calypso Monarch Competition and several other bodies throughout the island have some form of competition at Carnival time. Competition and the calypsonian seem therefore destined to maintain their long-standing relationship, though most of the recognized top calypsonians and former kings/monarchs have withdrawn from competing with the claim that there is nothing else to prove or to attain, but also, one suspects, with the nagging feeling that losing is something that they, their fans and their prestige would find most unpalatable.

The Road March

In many respects, the Road March is the people's competition, their chance to show "the judges" what a good, peppy calypso really is. In 1974, for example, many patrons at the Dimanche Gras Show felt that the Mighty Shadow should have won with his "Bassman" as the main contender. Over the ensuing Carnival days, the populace enthusiastically made "Bassman" the Road March in a show of popular justice. However, for the Road March the emphasis is on melody as opposed to lyric, and Carnival revelry and the Roach March go hand in hand.

The modern practice of the Road March is seen by Errol Hill to have been derived from the Kalinda, an early type song that accompanied stick-fighting. "It was chanted in the canboulay procession and has furnished the basic pattern for numerous roadmarch calypsoes."[44] It is also associated with the "lavway" (derived from the French *la voix*, meaning "the voice")" especially composed for chanting on the streets by a band of masqueraders."[45] The lavway, the "leggo" (from "let go") and the "breakaway" still set people dancing at Carnival parties and naturally spill over into the two-day Carnival parade.

The Road March is the calypso that, by popular acclaim, is played/sung by the majority of the Carnival bands over the two days of Carnival.[46] As such, it can never be decided before Carnival, though the leading contenders are all rehearsed by the orchestras, both "brass" and steelband, during the pre-Carnival season. This had led to accusations by some calypsonians that the steelbands in particular favour the "big boys" and do not play their calypsoes "on the road." The 1960's and the 1970's saw Kitchener and Sparrow controlling the lion's share of the Road March scene. Kitchener, the acknowledged Road March King, winning the title some ten times since 1963 when he returned from England, is said to be very skilled at composing music "for the pan." He and Sparrow are helped by the fact that their songs are usually available on record much earlier, a situation that changed drastically in the late 1970's as the other calypsonians entered the record market in full array.

Ideally, the Road March has a very catchy tune, with a chorus that the revelers can sing *in toto* or in part. Sometimes, there is no one outstanding calypso and in such a case a simple numerical count is taken by the Carnival Development Committee officials at certain vantage points. The result is that certain revelers, depending on what section of the town they celebrate the Carnival, have the impression that a particular calypso is the Road March, whereas in fact it is another that is played more frequently elswehere. This is however accepted in good faith and one finds very little controversy over the choice of the Road March.

Calypso lyric and calypso melody

A good calypso is usually rememberd for one of two reasons: either the lyrics are outstanding or the melody is infectious. In the former case, it matters little that the melody cannot even be hummed correctly. What is said is so powerful that it stands on its own. In the latter, the lyrics are only incidental to the beauty of the tune. Most Road Marches fall into this latter category and the practice over the years has been for calypsonians to compose two types of calypsoes: one in more serious vein with a weaker melody, the other with little serious in the way of content, meant mainly to provide dance music over the Carnival season. Naturally, the truly outstanding and unforgettable calypso is the one that manages to combine both these elements with success.

It seems logical that the calypso should have evolved with more emphasis being placed on lyric than on melody, since its role as some sort of mouthpiece was almost predominant. However, tradition also overtook the melody. Errol Hill writes: "it is often alleged that for decades preceding the 1920's and 1930's calypsoes were composed around a certain fixed number of established tunes that were used repeatedly with subtle variations. Singers and string-band accompanists had a knowledge of sol-fa notation and most songs were pitched in one of four minor keys: Re minor, Mi minor... Sol minor and La minor." He further states that Atilla the Hun maintained in a public lecture in Port of Spain that there were only 12 basic calypso rhythms, which were used repeatedly.[47] Hollis Liverpool, in his study based on interviews with veteran calypsonians, discloses that in the 1930's and 1940's the same tune was used by many singers, who simply added lyrics to known melodies of the day.[48] This would indicate quite clearly that lyric was more important than melody.

This also meant the inevitable possibility for controversy—a factor that has dogged calypso to this day. It has opened the way for accusations of "thiefing" by many calypsonians, as a song suddenly finds itself with multiple parents or with one calypsonian claiming as his own a tune that everybody throughout the Caribbean knows to be part and parcel of the folklore of some island or islands. For example, both the Mighty Unknown and the Roaring Lion claim (along with "proof") that they composed the popular "Nettie, Nettie," and "Sly Mongoose" is said to have existed in many versions outside of Trinidad.

The Mighty Sparrow ushered in a new era for calypso melody, what with his myriad innovations in this domain and his constant blend with fine lyrics. Where the public was willing to accept a good lyric with a poor melody, or vice versa, Sparrow created the expectation of both these elements in happy union. He happens to be blessed with a finer voice than the average calypsonian—though the public does not hold quality of voice against any but the very worst—and so has set standards extremely high for those aspiring to emulate him.

The simple calypso in Mi minor, the key that was eventually predominant, gave way to more intricate compositions, in particular with the increasing incidence and popularity of calypsoes on record (Sparrow has released at least one Long-Playing record per year since 1957). In such a situation, there could be no question of using the same stock of melodies and things have now progressed to the point where the music arrangers are playing an increasing role in the success of the calypsonian. Capitalizing on the fact that a good melody can still "sell" a weak calypso lyric, the arrangers are using the full spectrum of the electronic advances to produce calypsoes that are very attractive from a musical point of view. Melody is no longer the neglected step-daughter.

Arrangers played a great part in one of the more controversial matters of the mid-to-late 1970's. In an attempt to introduce more variety and variation in his compositions, Lord Shorty, by his claim, sought to find the "soul of calypso" and thus coined the term "Soca," little realizing that he was about to trouble the proverbial hornet's nest. The new beat, masterly arranged by Ed Watson, who promptly claimed the "invention" to be partly his, was an instant hit with dance audiences and the controversy raged: Is Soca calypso? The purists, including the eloquent Roaring Lion, saw it as a decadent step for the calypso. The supporters saw it as just another of the

many dimensions adopted by the calypso over the years and cited the calypso rock, the calypso twist and the calypso disco. What is interesting for our
purposes, however, is that the lyrics have not changed at all. The same
topics are being treated, only in a new beat that calypsonian and arranger
found more commercially viable.

Calypsoes on record

Researchers in the field cite 1914 as the year that the calypso was first
recorded. The Victor Gramophone Company sent a technician to Trinidad
to record "Sly Mongoose" as played by Lionel Belasco, then the leading
musician and composer.[49] Errol Hill states that "in 1925 Columbia began
issuing calypso records, Okeh in 1927-1928 and Decca in 1934."[50] Eduardo
Sa Gomes had opened his Radio Emporium in 1930 and he too "arranged
for leading calypsonians of the day (among them the Roaring Lion and
Atilla the Hun) to be recorded by the American Record Corporation in
1934."[51]

The Second World War brought American servicemen to bases in
Trinidad and their presence accounted for a hitherto unseen vogue in the
entertainment industry and recordings were made in studios in the island.
The most noteworthy event of the immediate post-war period was the ob-
vious pirating of Lord Invader's "Rum and Coca Cola." The Andrews
Sisters made famous the words:

> Rum and Coca Cola
> Way down Point Cumana
> Both mother and daughter
> Working for the Yankee dollar

and they also made the money. It is alleged that record sales totaled some
five million copies worldwide and a copyright infringement suit was
brought against the company concerned. Lord Invader, in typical calypso
style, frittered away what money he won from the suit.

In the mid 1950's Harry Belafonte released a calypso album "which
literally shook the foundations of the music world and, to boot, sold many
millions of copies on the world recording market."[52] Trinidadians considered Belafonte a "Johnny-come-lately" who sang calypsoes in "good
English," but his contribution cannot be totally ignored. "The accompani-
ment of his calypsoes was technically and expertly arranged and executed by
highly efficient musicians. The lyrics were clear and quite understandable to
the American ears... All in all, it must be admitted that Belafonte has
helped in some measure to internationalize calypso."[53]

Meanwhile, Lord Kitchener had gone to England and kept a stream of
records coming back to Trinidad. He recorded with leading Trinidad musicians in exile, among them guitarist Fitzroy Coleman, and catered both to
his many fans back home and to the growing band of West Indian immigrants flocking to the "Mother Country" in search of employment.

The Mighty Sparrow inaugurated a new era in calypso recordings. By the mid 1950's the Long-Playing record was coming into its own and Sparrow made full use of it, even having his own recording company at one stage. Sparrow's supremacy in this field was immediately apparent as not many calypsonians could sustain an album with ten or twelve songs so regularly. Many only managed one "45" per season.

Emery Cook, with his Cook Recording Company, did many on-the-spot recordings in the 1950's. His records of in-tent picong, of Carnival revelry in the streets, even of Sparrow as he sounded on the night he won the crown in 1956 with "Jean and Dinah," have all become precious collectors' items.

The situation had now progressed to the point where at least a dozen new LP's were available for the 1979 Carnival record buying public, as were numerous 45's. This means that the calypsonian is forced to compose more material if he is to cash in on the growing market. In addition he has to work well ahead of the Carnival season so that all re-mixing, of which a lot is done abroad, and pressing can be completed in time. Even so, in 1980, calypsonians found themselves in the paradoxical situation of having recorded songs being clamoured for by the public but being unable to have records pressed because of inadequate manufacturing facilities.

Putting calypsoes on record has emphasized the commercialization of the art. Calypsonians not fortunate enough to have their own financial backing still complain of exploitation on the part of producers, tent managers and disc jockeys who, they claim, pass very little of the returns on to them. Not many of the calypsonians belong to any body that looks after copyright and royalty arrangements and as such are open victims for schemers. Both calypsonian and record producer must take into account the varying tastes of the market, saturated as it is with so much other material. Consequently, some calypsoes are aimed fairly and squarely at the buying public at Carnival time with the resultant loss of the "genuine" nature of some of these songs and the composition of rather stereotyped lyrics. Finally, hard-sell marketing techniques are being employed more and more as attempts are made to recoup initial financial outlays, since producing a record has become quite an expensive affair.

Records pre-suppose record players in homes, where modern electronic equipment makes technical excellence in recording imperative, or, failing that, air play on the radio. There is an on-going complaint by the calypsonians that their songs are not given sufficient exposure on the radio, save for the weeks prior to Carnival. "Play my music," pleaded the Warrior. "...On the shelf, like you want them to play theyself," commented the Mighty Duke about the fate of many of the calypsoes. The situation has shown marked improvement over the years, but even today, in the "Land of the Calypso," as the Government-owned National Broadcasting Service reminds its listeners every night as it ends its transmission, calypsoes account for less than 25% of songs aired during the non-Carnival months of the year.

Calypso outside Trinidad

As we have seen, records helped to give the calypso an international audience. Calypsonians have themselves taken the calypso abroad and in many instances several have remained outside of Trinidad, wherever it was possible either for them to live solely from calypso or to make a living in some field, thereby allowing them the opportunity to compose and sing calypsoes as they wished.

Various metropolitan centres (Toronto, New York, London...) now have mini-Carnivals at some stage during the year and both locally resident and Trinidad resident calypsonians take part in the accompanying Calypso Competitions. Similarly, many calypsonians from the other Caribbean islands make the annual trek to Trinidad to appear in the tents, but they have been debarred from competing in the National Monarch Competition. In many instances, they work with the same Trinidad musicians and arrangers and as a result produce material that is almost indistinguishable from that done exclusively in Trinidad. The islands also have their Carnivals and Trinidad calypsonians participate in the accompanying competitions (Chalkdust was at one stage Calypso King of the Virgin Islands).

The trek to Trinidad at Carnival time is also made by Trinidadian calypsonians in self-imposed exile who, like Lord Nelson, return to renew their inspirations. These are the country's unofficial "ambassadors" who keep the calypso flag flying throughout the year when, even in Trinidad, the calypso is not being given the attention it deserves.

Calypsonian and calypso singer

The difference between the two is one of authenticity, according to Lord Pretender and Lord Superior.[54] This same difference is maintained by Black Stalin, who refers to the authentic practitioner of the art as the kaisonian and to the mere singer of calypso as the calypsonian. Most people are not aware of, or care very little about, any presumed difference.

Calypsonians singing calypsoes they had not composed are not new. Lord Beginner relates how he gave songs to other calypsonians in the early days and many middle class creole whites composed songs in the 1920's that they gave to their favourite bards. This practice has persisted throughout the years, with some prominent non-calypsonian composers (Rocky McCollin and Nelson Caton, for example) supplying popular calypsoes for both recognized and debutant, and with some calypsonians (Chalkdust, Shorty and Explainer among them) continuing to give songs to colleagues. Some composers who merely supplied calypsoes to others have lately started to sing their own songs (the Merchant, for example).

If, then, this practice has been going on for years, why all the fuss about "singing other people song?" It seems to stem directly from the annual competitions, in which points are awarded for "originality." Lord Superior has campaigned continuously to have two separate competitions, arguing that it is unfair to judge on the same level one who has composed both lyric and melody and who has then performed his own calypso alongside one who merely renders someone else's efforts. The former, according to Superior, is a calypsonian, the latter a calypso singer.

The other reason for the fuss is a more human one—a simple matter of professional jealousy. By tradition, calypsonians will not sing calypsoes already done by others unless they specialize in such for night club purposes (the Mighty Robin), or, do so at a special show honouring the greats. Even the popular live performance routine of imitating outstanding colleagues is something only Sparrow and Relator seem to do well (they both do a creditable Kitchener). The calypsonian, then, must at all times appear to be 100% original. Failing this, his prestige is somewhat tarnished. For example, there have been rumours for years that Sparrow receives help with his compositions, a fact he manages somehow not to confirm or deny. In fact, in his pique over losing the Calypso King Competition in 1961, Sparrow accused the Carnival Development Committee of choosing as King "a man with no originality." It is however no real secret that he does work in collaboration with at least one composer, Winsford Devine, who can produce his royalty statement from the Society for the Performing Arts to substantiate his claim to authorship, though "claim" might not be the term to use, since Devine maintains that he has a good working relationship with Birdie and is quite happy to see Sparrow have all the acclaim.[55]

There is one final implication of the calypsonian/calypso singer issue, one that concerns us directly in this study. When, for example, we say that Sparrow takes a particular stand on a point, is it really Sparrow? Are we in fact quoting Explainer? Or Singing Francine? How can we speak of the philosophy of a calypsonian when he might only be a voice singing someone else's calypso? The answers to these very pertinent questions lie, it would seem, in the overall approach to calypso by the Trinidad public, which, by and large, does not really care who did the actual composing. The calypsonian is accepted at face value. Calypsoes are inextricably associated with the calypsonians presenting them. As a result, what remains in the mind of the public is what came from the mouth of the calypsonians themselves. It is truly a case of "If Sparrow say so, is so," as he boasted very early in his career. In its own way, the Trinidad public has made the hidden composer issue a very academic matter by not seriously bothering with it, by willingly ignoring it once the calypsonian pleases in his performance. Whoever first sings a calypso publicly has authorship bestowed on him and there the matter rests.

This, then, is the situation at present. The calypso has had an eventful evolution and will no doubt continue to evolve, though the process might be slowed down somewhat as a result of all the attention being paid to the art form. Drastic changes will be fewer once processes become more formalized. Evolution is, in a way, assured for the simple reason that no art form can remain static and survive.

NOTES

[1]Fedo Blake, "Our Own Calypso: Its Birth, Revolution," *Sunday Guardian,* 29 January 1978, pp. 19-20.

[2]Helen Russell, *West Indian Scenes* (London: Hale, 1942), p. 203.

[3]Errol Hill, *The Trinidad Carnival* (Austin: University of Texas Press, 1972), pp. 60-61.

[4]Ibid.

[5]The plural is shown as either "calypsos" or "calypsoes." The latter is used throughout this study, except where the former is part of a quotation.

[6]A derivative from the French "chanterelle." It is spelt variously "shantwell," "chantwelle," "chantuel."

[7]Andrew Pearse, "Mitto Sampson on Calypso Legends of the Nineteenth Century," *Caribbean Quarterly*, Vol. IV, Nos. 3 & 4 (March/June 1956), p. 253.

[8]Hill, p. 57.

[9]See Pearse, op. cit.

[10]Gordon Rohlehr, "The Development of the Calypso, 1900-1940," Mimeographed article, 1972, p. 3. Subsequently published in *Tapia* as "Forty Years of Calypso." *Tapia*, Vol. 2, Nos. 1, 2 & 3 (September/October), 1972.

[11]See Andrew Pearse, "Carnival in Nineteenth Century Trinidad," *Caribbean Quarterly,* Vol. IV, Nos. 3 & 4 (March/June 1956), pp. 175-193; Bridget Brereton, "The Trinidad Carnival 1870-1900," *Savacou,* Nos. 11/12 (September 1975), pp. 46-57; Errol Hill, op. cit.

[12]Rohlehr, p. 2.

[13]"Jamet" (also and more frequently "Jamette") is derived from the French "diamètre," meaning "diameter." It means an underworld type, one beneath the "diameter" of social respectability.

[14]Brereton, op. cit., p. 47. My emphasis.

[15]Rohlehr, pp. 3-4.

[16]Hill, p. 64.

[17]Errol Hill, "The Calypso," in Anthony & Carr (eds.), *David Frost introduces Trinidad and Tobago* (London: André Deutsch, 1975), pp. 77-78.

[18]Hill, *The Trinidad Carnival*, p. 65.

[19]Errol Hill in *Trinidad Guardian*, 11 February 1968, p. 3.

[20]Rohlehr, p. 11.

[21]Hill, *The Trinidad Carnival*, p. 65.

[22]See Hollis Liverpool, "From the Horse's Mouth," Unpublished Caribbean Studies Thesis, U.W.I., St. Augustine, 1973.

[23]Hill, p. 77.

[24]In *Sunday Express*, 25 February 1979.

[25]Hill, p. 78.

[26]Hill, pp. 73-74.

[27]Janheinz Jahn states that "the name has been Caribbeanized by changing the two t's for two l's." In *Neo-African Literature: A History of Black Writing* (New York: Grove Press, 1968), p. 178.

[28]See Note 7.

[29]Personal communication with author, 17 October 1979.

[30]See Liverpool, op. cit.

[31]Hill, p. 58.

[32]See Note 7.

[33]Hill, p. 58.

[34]Elma Reyes, "Women hold their own in Kaiso World," *Trinidad Express*, February 1979.

[35]Ibid.

[36]Ibid.

[37]Rohlehr, p. 8.

[38]Hill, p. 64.

[39]See Liverpool, p. 5.

[40]Ibid., p. 25.

[41]Ibid.

[42]Ibid., p. 70.

[43]The Carnival Development Committee's point scheme for the Calypso Monarch Competition 1980 was: Lyrics 30, Melody 30, Rendition 15, Originality 15 and Presentation 10.

[44]Hill, p. 70.

[45]Hill, p. 60.

[46]In 1955 a North American ballad "The Happy Wanderer" was the Road March. This has not happened since.

[47]Hill, p. 72. He probably meant "melodies."

[48]Liverpool, p. 35.

[49]*Sunday Express*, Progress Supplement, 29 April 1979, p. 8.

[50]Hill, p. 56.

[51]*Sunday Express*, loc. cit.

[52]*Sunday Guardian,* 5 February 1978, p. 7.

[53]Ibid. The question of clarity is of no small importance once calypsonians think of extending their market beyond the Caribbean. Sparrow, for example, recorded two versions of "The Village Ram," the second having more "intelligible" lyrics and more "correct" English.

[54]Personal communication with author.

[55]Personal communication with author. Sparrow is also reported to have admitted in a television interview that he collaborated with Reggie "Piggy" Joseph.

2
THE LANGUAGE OF THE CALYPSO

The modern calypsonian is the sum of many traditions, any of which may surface from time to time. Observers seeking a clear-cut and exact definition of the calypso must constantly bear this fact in mind, since the calypsonians reach back into what became the oral tradition of which they are part and use elements of it either singly or in conjunction with others.

The first two decades of this century saw the definitive conversion from patois to English, though it seems clear that songs in English had existed before then. Mitto Sampson quotes a song by a white chantwell, Cedric Le Blanc, on the reprehensible conduct of the female chantwell Bodicea in 1873:

It was shocking to see, it was shameful to see
Carnival in the cemetery
It couldn't happen in Grenada
St. Kitts, Martinique or Antigua
When such lawlessness can prevail
Tell me what's the use of the Royal gaol

Bodicea the jamette who we all know
Is a real disgrace to we Cariso
I really can't understand
Why she didn't take the training of the Englishman
Roaming all about the vicinity
Cat and dog passing they mouth on she
Is better she die or lock up in jail
She disgrace every woman in Port of Spain.[1]

It is likely that this was not an isolated case, since the British by that time were well into their drive to educate the colonials. As a result, the claim by Lord Executor that another Le Blanc introduced calypsoes in English in 1898:

From abolition to ninety-eight
Calypso was still sung in its crude state
From French to English it was then translated
By Norman Le Blanc who became celebrated
Then it was rendered grammatically
In oration, poetry and history[2]

29

may not be entirely accurate, though it does provide a convenient reference
point. In fact, there is another claim. Errol Hill states that he was informed
that credit was due to Senior Inventor, who duly boasted:

> If they ask you for me
> Tell them I, Inventor, come
> Tell them I come to teach them
> Some English calypso.[3]

What does seem certain, then, is that the calypso was undergoing a period
of transition.

If we can go back to the Cedric Le Blanc "cariso" for a while, we note
that, already, the English used shows signs of Trinidad creolese. "They
mouth" is used instead of "their mouth" and "on she" instead of "on
her." Non-standard or Trinidad English was to become the only accepted
form in the calypso, with the use of standard or "good" English relegated
to the odd occasion. Of course, a mixture of standard and non-standard
English provides the calypsonian with a wider range of rhyming possibilities
and it is not ususual to see the calypsonian use "on she" in one verse and
"on her" in another, depending on what his rhyming needs were. Still,
scarcely a year goes by without the outcry against the language used in the
calypso. Witness this letter from a "Trini-American" resident in Brooklyn
to the editor of one of the Trinidad newspapers:

> The Editor: Now that the Carnival season is fast ap-
> proaching, I expect to hear better calypsoes sung, par-
> ticularly with regard to the language used. I always
> wondered why calypsoes have to be sung in broken
> English. I don't know, but I feel calypsoes can be sung in
> proper English and still sound good.
>
> For instance, children growing up today try to imitate
> certain calypsonians; and eventually, they begin to speak
> badly. So, from now on, let us try to make our calypsoes
> nicer and more appreciative, with proper English composi-
> tions.
>
> When our calypsonians go abroad, the foreigners do not
> understand what they are singing and keep asking Trinida-
> dians to interpret. That is why I am urging that proper
> English be used.[4]

Another writer to the same newspaper observed: "Even Sparrow, that most
tuneful of calypsonians, seems sometimes in difficulty to sing a rhyme
without expressions like 'gi she' and 'tell he.'"[5] To be fair, these criticisms
are not leveled solely at the calypsonians, since the "good English/bad
English" debate has been a live issue for many years.

The quotation from Lord Executor contains an interesting assertion:
"...it was rendered grammatically." This would seem to be in sharp con-
trast to what the calypsonians went on to do with their use of Trinidad

creole, but "grammatically" must be seen here as a concern for basic English, as opposed to patois, and in particular for its wide range of vocabulary. Gordon Rohlehr comments on the patois-to-English changeover toward the end of the nineteenth century: "The struggle for language was particularly painful. Before the patois-speaking pupil accommodated himself to speaking and writing in English, he had to relate the new language to the rhetorical traditions of the old one." He further notes the observations of an Education official of the time: "Collens noted that many of his secondary school pupils were intrigued by the sound rather than by the sense of words. Indeed, they seemed to be interested in words for their own sake, rather than as vehicles for communicating meaning."[6] This concern for the sound of words has survived to the present time in the calypso and was especially evident during the oratorical calypso and the calypso wars. The following example of word intoxication comes from a duet between Atilla the Hun and the Roaring Lion "pillorying a local character...who was notorious for his use of extravagant language:"

Lion

On grammatical subjects I will now state
Inviting lexicographers who can debate
With Ramsomfousis asceticism
They may try to argue but are bound to run
Through the extensive alteration of anklyosis
And my encyclopaedic analysis
That makes me a man of psychology
And I can always sing grammatically

Atilla

From the very moment that you commence
You are singing nothing but arrant nonsense
You have your listeners in dismay
They can't understand a single word you say
You're trying to indulge in phraseology
And only demonstrating stupidity
For you are no man of psychology
And you will never sing grammatically.[7]

It is evident that meaning is subordinate to sound and dexterity of delivery, and Sparrow, parodying this love for extravagant language, even goes as far as to allow sound to take over completely, with only an initial hint at meaning. In his "Well-Spoken Moppers," he castigates all those who "like to use words that's big and long," but who, unfortunately, are not aware that "they using them wrong." His so-called friends, after partaking of his hospitality, propose toasts to him at his home:

Here's to my good friend, I wish that he
And everybody live in enemity

> I wish him ill health and adversity
> Disaster and strife eternally
>   . . .
> May your cup of sorrow never run dry
> May misfortune follow you until the day you die
> You are such a nice quiet illiterate lad
> Your obnoxious company makes me feel glad
>   . . .
> May his friends bring him joy and frustration
> Impose on him and lift him to degradation
> He's a jolly good fellow and a kind reprobate
> Unscrupulous and always inconsiderate.

The amusing climax of this series of word juggling is that when the calypsonian tries to evict the "well-spoken" friends from his house, his wife comes
to their rescue, claiming that it was all a joke. She thus berates her husband:

> Pompomloomically speaking you're a pussyistic man
> Most elaquitably full of shitification
> Your splendiferous views are too catsarstical
> Too cuntimoratic and too bitchilistical.

The ear perceives certain key words at the beginning of Sparrow's
neologisms but apart from these he uses pure nonsense words—high-
sounding and impressive to those obsessed with such verbal acrobatics. This
is one tradition that has been kept throughout the evolution of the calypso
into its present form, though it obviously does not appear in every song.
When it does, however, it is immediately recognized and appreciated. This
concern for language permeates Trinidad society and is reflected in the constant love for picong, heckling and "fatigue," as well as for puns, word
play and *double entendre*. The calypsonian, in capturing these elements in
his song, captures that which is close to the very heart of the society.

The use of English in the calypso did not at first mean that new forms
were conceived to suit the new language. In fact, it is clear that the calypsoes
in English were merely versions of established patois forms. One such form
was the kalinda from stick-fighting, "belligerent in character, sung in one-
line or two-line verse and chorus pattern."[8] This form of calypso, the call-
and-response, is the one that has been associated most closely with the Road
March, for which it is admirably suited. The call-and-response technique is,
of course, not exclusive to the kalinda or the calypso and is in fact to be
found in many other areas, notably the spiritual, gospel song and the
worksong. Sparrow resorted to this form in what turned out to be an eloquent instance of self defense. Accused of wounding with intent, he literally
took his case to the people. Whether or not this accounted for his acquittal
will never be known for sure, but the resultant calypso "Ten to One, is
Murder" has become a much-quoted classic which bears repetition here.
Sparrow begins by setting the scene, talking about the unnamed "they:"

> Well, they playing bad
> They have me feeling sad
> Well, they playing beast
> Why they run for Police

Sparrow: Ten criminals attack me outside of Miramar
Chorus: Ten to one is murder
Sparrow: About ten in the night on the fifth of October
Chorus: Ten to one is murder
Sparrow: Way down Henry Street by H.G.M. Walker
Chorus: Ten to one is murder
Sparrow: Well the leader of the gang was hot like a pepper
Chorus: Ten to one is murder
Sparrow: And every man in the gang had a white-handle razor
Chorus: Ten to one is murder
Sparrow: They say ah push they girl from Grenada
Chorus: Ten to one is murder
Sparrow: Well ah back back until ah nearly fall in the gutter
Chorus: Ten to one is murder
Sparrow: You could imagine my position, not a police in the area
Chorus: Ten to one is murder.

The second stanza centres on his reaction to the attack. Cleverly, Sparrow shows no sign of participation on his part, save involuntary sweating:

> Well, ah start to sweat
> Man, ah soaking wet
> Mama, so much threat
> That's a night ah can't forget

The call-and-response continues in the same vein and leads us to the final stanza, which only restates the situation, his and "theirs," and leaves the climax to the very last line where, again cleverly, he avoids implicating himself in any wrongdoing. Who, after all, can blame him for "hearing" an explosion?:

Sparrow: But ah get away and ah run till ah reach Johnson corner
Chrous: Ten to one is murder
Sparrow: They take off in mih skin with big stick and boulder
Chorus: Ten to one is murder
Sparrow: The fella in front was a very good pelter
Chorus: Ten to one is murder
Sparrow: Ah hear 'potow pow' and the crowd start to scatter
Chorus: Ten to one murder.

The kalinda form was never used by Sparrow so openly again, though it can be detected in many of his compositions, evidence of the survival of that tradition within the society. Lord Melody had used it exclusively in his "Turn back, Melody," where the entire calypso is one of call-and-response (it even contains an apparent allusion to Sparrow's incident: 'You must be

think ah stupid like Sparrow'):
Chorus: Turn back, Lord Melody, turn back
Melody: Ah go fight dem, ah go fight dem
Chorus: Turn back, Lord Melody, turn back
Melody: Well dey playing bad but dey hungry
Chorus: Turn back, Lord Melody, turn back
Melody: Ah go kill de fus' man dat lash me
Chorus: Turn back, Lord Melody, turn back.

And Lord Kitchener, whose music is so infectious, usually makes use of the call-and-response technique in his Road March-type calypsoes, actually allowing the chorus—the response—to carry a fair share of the calypso. His 1976 Road March "Flag Woman" provides an example of this:

Kitchener: You have no band without a beautiful flag woman
           You have no band without an experience flag woman
           The band will have no control
           The rhythm will have no soul
           The revelers couldn't play
           The usual mas on Carnival day
Chorus: A woman really have the touches to send you bumping
           Sure to get you in her clutches when she start waving
           When you see she get that fever is plenty trouble
           Whether you are saint or sinner you bound to wiggle
Kitchener: Ay ya yai ya yai ya yai...
Chorus: Wave it baby
           Get them groovy
           Yes honey
           Do your duty
           Wave it sexy
           Send them crazy
           Woman, woman, move you' hand.

The entire chorus is sung without Kitchener except for his interjection in the middle as a sort of prod.

Another type of calypso that formed part of the oral tradition is the ballad, which has evolved into one of the main forms of the contemporary calypso. Mention could also be made of the belair, but it is here treated as essentially the forerunner of the ballad. Indeed, Errol Hill's description of the belair could fit many modern calypsoes quite well:" ...the belair was a more general song type used for a variety of purposes. The music was more lyrical than the calinda; the verses were longer, of four, six or eight lines with a chorus of two or four lines. The belair could be a song of praise or satire on an individual or a group; it could be a witty or humorous commentary on topical events; or it could record personal adventures, real or imagined, amorous or otherwise."[9] The Roaring Lion has consistently maintained that the calypso is a "ballade" and sees it having its roots all the way back to François Villon, the fifteenth century French poet who specialized in this form. Chieftain Douglas is credited with the introduction of the ballad in calypso, having as his main input his narrative ability: "he carefully plotted his story in order to emphasize crucial details as well as to heighten the element of suspense."[10] This description, along with that of the belair given earlier, could encompass the majority of today's calypsoes.

With such complexity and richness of background, it goes without saying that the contemporary calypso can at any time be a combination of many styles and forms. The most basic form consists of 3 or 4 eight-line stanzas followed by a chorus/refrain that varies from two to eight or ten lines, depending on the impact the calypsonian is seeking to achieve. (Recording restrictions forced a reduction in the previous high number of stanzas.) The chorus/refrain is sung by the calypsonian alone, in combination with a back-up group or entirely by this group. In many instances, the first two of the eight lines are repeated, giving in fact a six-line stanza in terms of composition. There seems to be no hard and fast rule governing the use of repetition, save the fact that the repeated initial couplet ensures that the calypsonian has his audience in full control, not unlike the repetition used by the preacher. One notices, however, that there can be a slight variation in the repetition, once again to establish the close "ole talk" feeling with the listener. In Sparrow's "Wahbeen and Grog"

> Something on you' mind ah want to know
> Darling why you behaving so

is repeated as

> Something on you' mind ah want to know
> Sparrow why you behaving so.

Similarly, in his "Take You' Bundle and Go"

> A man come back home from a meeting
> Catch he wife with a next man cheating

is repeated as

> This fella came home from a meeting
> Catch he wife with a next man cheating

(Note also the two forms of the past: "come" in the first couplet and "came" in the second.)

Four and six-line stanzas are also used along with the chorus. Again, there seems to be no technical reason or pre-determined form which would make the calypsonian use the four-line or the six-line stanza, the use of one or the other depending entirely on the whim of the calypsonian. The search for innovation and variety over the years has led on occasion to the five-line and the seven-line stanza and to the absorption of the chorus/ refrain into the body of the stanza, making it difficult to say where one ends and the other begins. The following example by Sparrow shows to what extent the verse has been extended to engulf the chorus, leaving the music to provide the pause after the end of the stanza:

Contrary to yesterday
When wealth was a social law
The official concern today
Revolves around the poor
The sexual fancies and wild emotions
Unemployment, education, ethnic composition
Have now become interesting studies
Of exhaustive attention
While the rich become jealous
Cannot live with this rejection
They would like to be the object of concern
But idleness has no value of its own
Their methodology of conspicuous consumption and waste
Display of diamonds and rubies now commonplace
For the theory today is that wealth in its sphere
Is a source of destruction, frustration and fear
For the wealthy life is built on despair.

Admittedly, this is unusual and perhaps only a Sparrow could bring it off in song, but the case is noteworthy and one is reminded of the same polysyllabic structure mocked by Sparrow himself in "Well-Spoken Moppers" and a later stanza talks about the wealthy woman's "obesity...advanced nymphomania and repellent grace." This particular calypso contains two other stanzas of similar length and is one that really forces the listener to pay attention to every line. There is no relaxation as we come to a repeated chorus, only the musical pause before the start of the following stanza. It is equally interesting to observe that each stanza does in fact start off with half of what seems to be an ordinary eight-liner:

Stanza 2: Once upon a time
           People only had to know
           That you had more than just a dime
           To make of you a hero
                ...

Stanza 3: It is sad when a high-class broad
           Ravaged by gross ill health
           Throw she pride overboard
           Then combine in her rank and wealth

but subject matter and verbal dexterity take over.

As can be seen from the quotations used so far, calypsoes use rhyme or assonance, either, and for the most part, in the AA BB or the AB AB pattern. Poetic license is sometimes stretched to the limit to make words rhyme. Hence, "pregnant" is made to rhyme with "cent" "gallows" with "business" (by Lord Melody) or, as has been pointed out already, the interchange of standard and Trinidadian English can produce "tell her" for a rhyme with "order" or "tell she" for a rhyme with "city." Needing a word to rhyme with "party," Poser simply coined "warty" (apparently, in context, a marijuana joint). The internal rhyme is also to be found, as in Sparrow's

> Ah diggin' horrors Ah diggin' de blues
> Anytime I choose to peruse the daily news,

or Chalkdust's

> Just be aware that up there
> Is sex bare they want to hear,

or Squibby's

> Ah want a man, a man who could jam i-an (iron)
> Ah tell she I am the man, I am the champion
> And ah come down from I-an land, Oh Jeezan.

However simple, then, the calypso is a form of poetry and the better calypso is the one that evokes and maintains, beyond the mere topic, the charm of the poet. The calypsonian uses metre as a base and not as a trap, establishing just enough of a pattern to make us aware of its presence and to cause the listener to increase his attention. In this domain, Sparrow has done the most to free himself from the constraint of metre by sheer timing and skillfulness of delivery. "In Sparrow," comments Gordon Rohlehr, "metre exists as a powerful force which the singer cannot afford to ignore, but which he needs to conquer and against which he must establish such rhythmic patterns as the sense of what he is saying demands."[11] As a result, written transcription of many of Sparrow's calypsoes would tend to have the reader believe that the metre is non-existent. The ear, however, hears otherwise, perceives the poet—master of the word—in action. A final quotation is in order to "justify" the calypso aspiration to poetry: "...it is in the art of poetry and its immense verbal variability that individual talent flowers. For the poem is carried by the voice. It is sung or chanted, on specific occasions, some of which are part of specific rites and occupations... The most significant fact is that the ultimate realization of this material lies in the *occasion* and *atmosphere* of its performance."[12]

The calypsonians are constantly delivering this poetry to an audience as is evidenced by the frequent interlocutory interjections that they use to cement their rapport with their listeners. This rapport, we have seen, at times begins with the repetition of the initial couplet, assuring that the audience is in fact paying rapt attention. Thereafter, the calypsonian holds this attention in a variety of ways, some of which have become personal signatures of the calypsonian. The Mighty Spoiler punctuated his stanzas with "This is the Spoiler... Ah want to fall..." and even when later calypsonians openly imitated him (the Mighty Bomber, for instance), they too used the interjection "Ah want to fall." Sparrow has used a wide range of these over the years: "Let me tell you," "Whey you talking," "Don't doubt me," "Listen to the gospel," plus various cries: "Woopseemama," "Ah *yee* ha..." Further, he usually comes in over the chorus, sung or instrumental and particularly on record, with questions or comments. In "Congo Man," after maintaining that he "never eat a white meat yet," asks the players in the orchestra: "All you believe that, eh? A man like me...travel all about..." and completes this interjection with a laugh that can only be described as saucy. "Ah lie?" is used frequently by calypsonians to challenge audience acceptance of the bit of news or gossip being presented. Chalkdust punctuates his verses with what he calls his war cry:

> Until I die, they'll hear my cry
> 'Juba doo bai.'

Like Sparrow's "Woopseemama," it has no "meaning" and is just an utterance, half onomatopoeia, half jazz scat, a procedure the Mighty Shadow has taken to using in his calypsoes with his "Dum bay lai lai" and others. Lord Funny, who was one of the Spoiler imitators and who, despite his sobriquet, keeps his facial expression one of studied seriousness while he sings the most humorous of lines, uses a well-timed "Yes" and "Ah tell you," taken straight from "ole talk" and gossip. Sometimes, the interjection is nothing more than a naughty laugh, as is the case with Lord Blakie or with Kitchener, for example, in his "Little Drummer Boy" where he is relating how various women are impressed with his skill at "drumming." Kitchener's laugh between verses convinces the listener that his words are indeed loaded with *double entendre*. These and other devices—facial and body gesture—help to maintain the atmosphere of story-telling and calypsonian/audience interchange. They fit neatly into the overall presentation and help to make of the calypso a living genre that is appreciated on the spot by the audience for which it is created.

It is not at all unlikely that, of the many traditions that combine to make up the contemporary calypso, the West African *griot* also plays his part as distant forerunner or influence. Of the *griot* Dorothy Blair writes:

> In West Africa the *griots* were the story-tellers, chroniclers, praise-singers, poets, professional entertainers. A basic knowledge of the techniques and conventions of the recitals was as much a part of their stock-in-trade as the content of their narratives. Both "libraries" and skills would be transmitted from father to son in caste. To these, the narrators would add new elements inspired by their own individual gifts—unexpected imaginative details to surprise and delight were introduced among the well-known traditional features. Some specialized in realistic descriptions; some in complex, refined courtly poetry; some inspired awe and admiration by their eloquence in recounting noble, heroic exploits; some diverted by their comic burlesque, colloquial language or bawdy episodes.[13]

It is clear from the outset that the calypsonian is *not* the same as the *griot*.

There is, for example, no father to son transmission of skills and information, but the *griot* did have in his traditional bag several elements that could have survived the Middle Passage with the sturdy slaves. One therefore notes with interest the claim that the *griot* would add "unexpected imaginative details to surprise," that he would amuse with "colloquial language and bawdy episodes," and that he would "inspire awe by his eloquence." Let us examine these aspects of the *griot*'s craft as implicated in the language of the calypso.

On the question of imaginative details that surprise, the calypsonian very often holds back one crucial piece of information until the end, thereby changing the whole meaning of the calypso. A favourite procedure is the dream. The calypsonian has a series of adventures, only to discover in the final verse that he was dreaming. Sparrow's "Mr. Herbert" tells about an over-zealous lover whose female mate cannot cope with him. Finally,

> It happen so Herbert had to move
> From the place his time was up
> So no more trouble at all in the place
> And all the bacchanal stop
> Then suddenly something happen
> Ah find myself with mih eye open
> Well is now ah feeling bad
> How you don't know is a nightmare the Sparrow had.

His "Sailing Boat Experience" has him cast on the proverbial desert island, only this time he has 2,024 women to keep him company:

> Sparrow was in so much trouble
> Something hold me in mih navel
> Ah praying to see somebody
> So they could come and help me
> Then somebody touch mih shoulder
> It was mih wife Emelda
> Wake up, saga boy, stop dreaming
> It is ten o'clock in the morning

Chorus: I never had Mary Jane
> Everything seem to go in vain
> But mih wife in the house started to fret
> Sparrow, get up and get.

Another procedure has the calypsonian over-hearing a conversation in an adjoining room (not at all unlikely in the barrack-yard type of housing), with the final lines showing him verifying what is really taking place and justifying the *double entendre* to which the listener has been treated. These and other surprise endings are eagerly awaited as the calypsonian performs and he sometimes ends up saying that whole story was a joke or one big lie.

We have already seen how extensive use is made of colloquial language and the whole issue of "bawdy episodes" will be treated in a subsequent

chapter. On the question of awe-inspiration through eloquence, listen to
one *griot* on his art:

> I am a *griot*. It is I, Djeli...master in the art of speech...
> We are sacks of words, we are sacks that hold secrets many
> centuries old. The art of speech has no secrets for us;
> without us the names of kings would fall into oblivion; we
> are the memory of men; by words we give life to exploits of
> kings for the young generations.[14]

The one aspect that is immediately striking is the boasting on the part of the
griot. He does in fact seek to inspire awe, and credibility. The contention
here is that this very stance has been maintained in the contemporary calypso, having survived and been handed down to the calypsonian via another
tradition, namely that of the Carnival character, the Midnight Robber.

The Midnight Robber made his appearance in the early twentieth century and remained a stock Carnival character until the 1950's when he
began to appear less and less, to the point where he is now the province of
the die-hards. The Robbers were notable for two factors. Firstly, their
costumes:

> ...a variety of fancy costumes of which the most
> representative style today is the Elizabethan doublet and
> breaches enriched with beading and braid, an enormously
> exaggerated and elaborated hat with fringed brim and a
> crown molded into some creature or edifice, and shoes
> usually in the form of an animal with moving eyes. The
> whole is set off with a flowing cape on which symbols of
> death and destruction are embroidered or painted. In his
> hand he carries a revolver and a wooden money-box in the
> shape of a coffin. A cartridge belt and more guns adorn his
> waist. A whistle, upon which he blows constantly, com-
> pletes his outfit.[15]

Obviously, the Midnight Robber set out to drive fear into the hearts of his
victims and many children were literally terrified out of their wits by this
"mas."

Secondly, the Midnight Robber needed a language to accompany all
this outward show of bravado. And so was born "robber talk," an unending stream of braggadocio, cockiness and empty threats:

> ...I brought hell to a run that cause Lucifer's wife to
> take things to heart and die in despair, then I came back to
> this civilized world with one million pound in solid virgin
> gold... I braved the sea, I pierced the jungle. I scale the
> mountain. I conquered the desert, and the last thing on
> earth I am going to do is rob the last breath that was place
> in you.[16]

This type of speech has so captured the imagination of the Trinidad public that it sees any similar stance and outward show of bravado and brag-gadocio, be it from the Head of State or from the lowly labourer, as nothing more than pure "robber talk," hence not to be taken too seriously. It is this language that the calypsonian has inherited in part—the boasting of the *griot* and the bravado of the Midnight Robber. As a result, many calypsoes glorify this stance and advocate a violence that the listener immediately recognizes as empty. Sparrow has quite a range of calypsoes that fall into the "robber talk" category. The following excerpt is from "Don't Touch Me:"

Well a man can't walk in town
With them criminals going round
Ah say a man can't walk in town
With them criminals going round
Yes they pick you' pocket, they stab you in you' back
If you try to make noise the whole gang attack
They beat you soft and bossie you with cough
Then the magistrate let them off

Chorus: I ain't meddling with nobody
Nobody shouldn't trouble me
I ain't making joke with nobody
They ain't bound to make joke with me
I ain't arguing with you, I ain't quarrelling with you
I can't fight on the whole
But if you lash me, may the Lord have mercy on you soul.

The picture of the silent misanthrope just waiting to pounce on anyone who dares touch him is one that is viewed as part of the role-playing the calypso-nian has assumed. It must be added, though, that many of these calypsoes were also reflections of popular reaction to the spate of hooliganism that af-fected Trinidad in the late 1950's and as such were fewer in the succeeding decades. In Sparrow's case, he has kept up a running war with "them," the unnamed hooligan element, a war, one might add, that is not totally un-justified on the personal level. Hence he sings in "Hangman Cemetery:"

Why they molesting me
Ah don't interfere with anybody
They jealousy wouldn't cease
But at least ah could live in peace
. . .
They jealous and they envy
And they planning to commit a felony
But tell them don't tackle me
Before ah end up in the Hangman Cemetery.

We note here the same threat to eliminate the enemy in the last line of the chorus similar to Lord Melody's threat to "follow in the footsteps of mih father, Alexander the Murderer." In another calypso, "Royal Jail," he commits himself to prison for what he is going to do to the "criminals:"

> I done tell mih friends and mih family
> Not to worry
> Any one them interfere with me
> Take it easy
> Don't worry to beg the jury
> Save the lawyer fee
> And if you have any mail
> Send it to me at the Royal Jail.

And open war is declared in "Renegades:"

> Ah band mih jaw and ah make up mih mind for them
> They ask for war so to solve it ain't no problem
> Their crude behaviour I don't approve
> They stepping outa they grove
> Renegades, Sparrow coming, so move.

We are a long way from the *griot* and not too far from the Midnight Robber, but the calypsonian's art form is without doubt the direct result of an evolutionary process where several disparate elements under an overall heading combined to produce something that his audience can recognize and appreciate.

Robber talk was naturally the order of the day during the calypso wars, where the calypsonians had to score instant success with their verbal ability. The following illustration is taken from the RBF record album "The Real Calypso, 1927-1946" which has a rare recording of a war between Executor, Caresser, Atilla and the Roaring Lion, though they were not really fighting among themselves, but were attacking calypsonian Houdini. Consequently, the four are in a concerted firing line aiming at the same target, so the war is really to see who can outdo whom:

Executor

> At last the hour of vengeance is at hand
> I am in the land
> The Lord Executor's word of command
> With my glittering sword in hand
> Tell Houdini this is the hour of destiny
> In this colony.

Caresser

> Those who boast Houdini can sing
> In my opinion they know nothing
> For it's all propaganda, deceit and pretense
> He hasn't got the shadow of intelligence
> The money that was spent on his slates and books
> Has not improved his manners and looks
> He has a good inclination by foreign education
> In this colony.

Atilla and Lion continue the war with words that would do any Midnight Robber proud:

Atilla

From the very first day I was born
Men like Houdini started to mourn
Monarchs wept and princes cried
When they saw this new star up in the sky
Astronomers in my horoscope state
He'll be proud, grand, illustrious and great
And they named me Atilla, the terror, the brutal conqueror
Master Mi Minor

Lion

The earth is a-trembling and a-tumbling
And the heavens are falling; and all
Because the Lion is roaring
My tongue is like the blast of a gun. When I frown
Monarchs want to bow down to the ground
Devastation, destruction, desolation and damnation
All these I'll inflict on insubordination
For the Lion in his power is like the Rock of Gibraltar.[17]

The calypso war saw the use of an expression that has fallen into disuse but evocation of which immediately brings these verbal battles to mind. The expression "sans humanité" (pronounced "sandeemaneetay) was used as a mixture of refrain, interjection and final verse, having no logical connection with the sense of the preceding lyric, used principally to top off the attack just delivered. According to Errol Hill, its origin is uncertain, though he conjectures that it is a patois translation of the Hausa "kaiso" which developed a parallel meaning of "you deserve no pity; it serves you right."[18] There was pressure to have the "meaningless" expression dropped and for a time it was replaced by the English "in this colony" which we see at the end of the interventions by Executor and Caresser quoted above. Calypsonians still retain in essence the sans humanité posture, even though the actual expression appears only occasionally in tributes to and performances by the older generation of calypsonians.

It should by now be apparent that the calypsonian's feel for language is well nurtured. Of course, all is not bravado and robber talk, as subsequent chapters will show. However, in whatever form or style, the calypsonian as folk poet and repository of the oral tradition shows a keen sense of language pattern and rhythm. Rising above the doggerel about which V.S. Naipaul spoke: "A hundred foolish travel-writers (reproducing the doggerel sung 'especially' for them) and a hundred 'calypsonians' in all parts of the world have debased the form,"[19] the better calypsonian is the one who, in swift strokes, creates an imagery that literally sticks in the mind of his audience, no matter how simple this might be or precisely because of this simplicity. One thinks, for example, of Spoiler's comparison of himself and his twin brother to "two tin of the same make of consensed milk," with the image of the bewildered shopper before rows of similar tins, or of the "professional" cake-sticker kissing Spoiler's wife and lingering like "chewing gum stick on to a warm piece of iron," an image any chewing gum lover, or hater, will have little difficulty conjuring up, or of Sparrow's Dotish Married Man pulling and tugging at his new wife "as if he get she in a sale at Kirpalani," with the indelible image of the mad scramble at the popular hardware store simply but effectively conveying the calypsonian's meaning. Any Trinidadian or resident of the lower Eastern Caribbean who has ever tried to tune in his radio at night will immediately seize the terseness, humour and sheer power of suggestion of Sparrow's criticism of his mother-in-law for "cutting in like a Spanish radio station," giving new life to a bit of imagery probably familiar to many. The outsider might not always catch the significance of the image, but the calypsonian works principally for his home audience. Indeed, having to "explain" for the outsider robs the calypso, like the good joke, of half of its initial impact.

The use of the home-grown aphorism also lends to the calypsonian's imagery a picturesque appeal. To the same dotish married man who had intended to change his bride into a new person, Sparrow offers the following bits of advice:

When you plant cassava you can't get fig

You put a hog in a palace it still remain a pig.

In this respect, therefore, the calypsonian captures the essence of the Trinidad "ole talk" and "lime" when friends spend their time out-doing one another in verbal imagery.

This type of imagery, the one that remains with the listener and makes of the calypso something of a classic, is not to be confused with the mundane one found in so many calypsoes. Hustlers (calypsonians who "hustle" the tourist dollar at popular resorts throughout the year) care little about refined imagery or even about refined calypso. "A favourite trick in hustling," says Hollis Liverpool, "is to know the lines by rote, but change a few words etc. to make the listener feel that it is being done extemporaneously."[20] In similar vein, the annual Carnival celebrations never fail to produce its crop of "women shaking they waist/ wining down the place," of "grabbing mih woman/jumping in a band," of "enjoying the bacchanal/for the Carnival. . ." This does not mean that the calypsoes are not good, since the melodies are usually bouncy—an important ingredient for Carnival revelry—only that in calypsoes of this sort language is playing a somewhat secondary role.

We have therefore seen what the calypsonian does with language as a result of the oral tradition of which he is part and of the many influences to which he is subjected, either consciously or unconsciously. The modern calypsonian, becoming more and more professional in his performance of the calypso, has also tended, more and more, to tailor his musical style to suit contemporary public taste. However, while public taste may change with each succeeding generation, the basic language of the calypso, as distinct from the music, such as we have just examined, will undoubtedly continue to be accessible, the way it has been up to the present time.

SPECIAL NOTE: There is as yet no universally accepted spelling for Trinidad creole, the language of all the calypsoes. Consequently, what appear to be inconsistencies in the spelling—my/mih, I/ah, dey/they, dey/their/there etc.—are only attempts to capture, without resorting to phonetic transcription, the phrasing of the calypsonian in a given calypso rendition.

NOTES

[1]Andrew Pearse, "Mitto Sampson on Calypso Legends of the Nineteenth Century," p. 261. The continuity of the rhyme seems to preclude a translation from French patois.

[2]Quoted in Errol Hill, *The Trinidad Carnival,* p. 55.

[3]Ibid., p. 60.

[4]*Trinidad Express,* 10 November 1977, p. 5.

[5]*Trinidad Express,* 25 December 1978, p. 5.

[6]Gordon Rohlehr, "The Development of the Calypso, 1900-1940," p. 10.

[7]Hill, p. 74.

[8]Ibid., p. 70.

[9]Ibid., pp. 71-72.

[10]Ibid., p. 66.

[11]Gordon Rohlehr, "Sparrow as Poet," p. 84.

[12]Kofi Awoonor, *The Breast of the Earth* (New York: Anchor Books, 1976), p. 90.

[13]Dorothy Blair, *African Literature in French* (Cambridge: Cambridge Univesity Press, 1976), p. 25.

[14]D.T. Niane, *Sundiata. An Epic of Old Mali* (London: Longmans, 1965), p. 1.

[15]Hill, pp. 90-91.

[16]Ibid., p. 19.

[17]From notes accompanying "The Real Calypso 1927-1946" (New York: RBF Records No. 13, 1966), p. 4. This transcript has been corrected in certain parts.

[18]Hill, p. 63.

[19]V.S. Naipaul, *The Middle Passage* (Harmondsworth: Penguin Books, 1969), p. 76.

[20]Hollis Liverpool, "From the Horse's Mouth," p. 13. Lord Pretender has also claimed that most of the "old timers" sang this type of "prepared extempo."

WELCOME TO TRINDIDAD Calypso

(C) (P) Sparrow Music
Produced by Trinity Music
5th Drive, Mount D'or Road
Champs Fleurs, Trinidad, West Indies

Composed by "The Mighty Sparrow"
Arranged by Tony Prospect

JOHNNY SPARROW
"THE MIGHTY SPARROW"

WELCOME TO TRINIDAD

CALYPSO

Composed by Sparrow

Arranged by Tony Prospect

Love - ly bea - ches and sun shine,

Right a - way you're in love...........

Lie on the sand, hear Ca -- lyp - so and ste

Band un - der blue skies a - bove.............

CHORUS

Wel - come to sweet Tri - ni - dad,

To have you here we're so glad..............

WELCOME   TO   TRINIDAD

VERSE   (1)

Lovely beaches and sunshine

Right away you're in love

Lie on the sand; hear Calypso and Steelband

Under blue skies above.

CHORUS

Welcome to sweet Trinidad

To have you here we are so glad

Please have a wonderful stay

Hope you will come back some day.

VERSE   (2)

Local dishes you must taste

Pig tail, Ochro and rice

Good pound Plantain, Cassava dumpling

Tell all you friends how it nice

VERSE   (3)

Visit St. Madeline and La Brea

Sleep in San Fernando

See the sugar that we make

See the Oilfields and Pitchlake

Spend a week-end in Tobago.

VERSE   (4)

Donkey race in Siparia

Tobago Goat race is fun

Sweet Shango drum, Limbo drink Rum

Have a wonderful time in the sun.

Black Stalin

The Mighty Spoiler

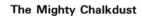
The Mighty Chalkdust

Brother Valentino

MANIA

Midday madness as 15,000 people throng Port of Spain's Woodford Square for lunch hour Calypso concerts.

HASELY CRAWFORD
Sparrow

Crawford
Like a bullet,
Take off like a jet,
Flash of lightning, he keep moving;
People bawling, everybody glad:
Is gold for Trinidad.

HASELY CRAWFORD
Brother Mudada

And if yuh hear we singing,
Yes, Hasley Crawford yuh is we idol,
Oh Lord yuh really show them yuh potential
What a living example,
To run for your people,
Bringing home a heavy gold medal
Ah hear that Uncle Sam
Want to claim we man
Saying dey a know,
He's a born Trinidadian.

GOLD
Maestro

Crawfie, we Crawfie,
Then they say they never see that yet:
Time to finish, moving like a jet.
Champion, Montreal, gold medal
Gold, Gold
The fastest human in the whole wide world
Gold — the man bring gold
The fastest human in the whole wide world

HASELY CRAWFORD
Striker

Trinidad, Trinidad
Believe me we more than glad
That you sent Hasely Crawford to the
twenty-first Olympiad
I was there and I saw
And I heard how the thousands roar
When the pistol burst
It was Hasely Crawford running down first

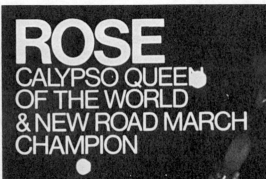

ROSE
CALYPSO QUEEN
OF THE WORLD
& NEW ROAD MARCH
CHAMPION

JUBA DUBAI

Chalkie keeps his crown

3
SOCIAL AND POLITICAL COMMENTARY IN THE CALYPSO

V.S. Naipaul has commented that "it is only in the calypso that the Trinidadian touches reality,"[1] thereby showing the other side of the picture which usually portrays the Trinidadian as seeking refuge from reality in Carnival and calypso. Indeed, many of the ills of contemporary Trinidad society are explained away by the statement that the people have a carnival or a calypso mentality, one that takes all too lightly matters of the utmost importance. Naipaul, himself a caustic critic of the foibles of Trinidad society, must have seen that beneath the ever-present tone of levity in the majority of calypsoes, the calypsonian constantly monitors what is happening around him and uses the platform of the calypso to expose to his listeners a point of view that is not only his personal one, but more often than not is indicative of what the man in the street is thinking about a particular situation. Because of the topical nature of most of the calypsoes that come under the banner of social and political commentary, it is obvious that these will be more easily appreciated on the home ground, whereas the other type of calypso—straight humour, fantasy or sexual escapade—has more universal appeal and popularity. This topical nature does not in any way mean that the calypsoes are devoid of interest to the outsider. On the contrary, one can follow the varying faces of Trinidad's social and political history through a careful analysis of many of the calypsoes composed over the years.

As we have seen in our examination of the language of the calypso, the contemporary calypsonian is part of a well-established tradition, a fact that is true of the area of social and political commentary as well. One of the earliest calypsoes in English was a reaction to the threat by the British to abolish the Port of Spain City Council in 1898. In his comment on this episode of Trinidad history, Eric Williams, wearing the historian's hat on this occasion, noted: "But Trinidad retaliated—*as so often the calypsonian being the mouthpiece*. Norman Le Blanc, Richard Coeur de Léon of calypso fame, immortalized Trinidad's resentment at the execution of the Port of Spain City Council:

> Jerningham the Governor
> It's a fastness into you

It's a rudeness into you
To break up the laws of the Borough Council."[2]
It is fitting that the historian should recognize the validity of the calypsonian as mouthpiece of popular feeling, since this same historian as politician
was to come in for his share of comment from the contemporary calypsonian and the ups and downs of his political career are well documented in
calypso.

There is, however, evidence that calypsoes—or at least the forerunners
of these songs—contained social commentary long before 1898. Historian
Bryan Edwards described the ability of slaves brought to the West Indies to
give full scope to a talent for ridicule "which is exercised not only against
each other but also, not unfrequently, at the expense of their owner or
employer."[3] These owners or employers were obviously not prepared to
tolerate this type of social protest from those who had no status in the society and whose songs were associated with a total lack of decency and respectability. The result was that by 1868 legislation was introduced prohibiting
the singing of songs deemed profane, with a number of convictions being
recorded against those who transgressed the law. This repression via convic-
tion *after* the calypsoes were performed led in later years to open censorship
in the 1930's when calypsonians were required to submit their compositions
for police scrutiny *prior* to their public performance, but "the order was
quickly rescinded in the face of mounting opposition."[4] In the interim, the
calypsonian seemed to have been victim of the double standard that was to
dog him even up to the present time: repression when it so moved the
authorities and acceptance when it suited their purpose. Fortunately, the
calypsonians stood their ground and continued to comment on whatever
they pleased, even on the fact that the calypso was being accused of being
"sacrilegious, obscene or profane." Atilla the Hun, who cemented the marriage of calypso and politics when he was elected to the City Council in
1946, and whose calypsoes "have been quoted in the Trinidadian House of
Assembly on several occasions,"[5] sang in response to the illogical and un-
justified censorship:

To say these songs are sacrilegious, obscene or profane
Is only a lie and a dirty shame
If the calypso is indecent, then I must insist
So is Shakespeare's Venus and Adonis
Boccaccio's tales, Voltaire's Candide
The Martyrdom of Man by Winwood Reid
Yet over these authors they make no fuss
But they want to take advantage of us.[6]

Atilla wanted to know "what those Englishmen know about calypso." He
touched on a fact of life in Trinidad, and in the Caribbean as a whole,
namely the all-too-ready acceptance of that which is foreign and the quasi-
total rejection of the indigenous. His point was well made and was to have

many supporters in later years whenever the problem of calypso content was raised, particularly, as we shall see in a later chapter, with respect to the "smutty" calypso.

Another politician of importance in the struggle against British colonialism, Albert Gomes, whose defeat marked the beginning of the era of the People's National Movement under Eric Williams, was an early champion of the calypso as a vehicle for social and political commentary. Though often the butt of much heckling himself, Gomes nevertheless recognized that:

> The Calypso is the most effective political weapon in Trinidad. The singers—all of them—are men reared in poverty and oppression, and they sing of the life they know. Thus it is that even when cleverly camouflaged with wit and banter, the sharp tang of social criticism is evident in their songs. Moreover, people go to the Calypso tents to be entertained. What politician, who must harangue from the rostrum, can boast of a better opportunity for influencing people's minds? The fact that the tents are so sedulously supervised by the police reveals the extent to which the Calypso singers influence political thought.[7]

Gomes' comment, coming as it did in the mid 1940's, must certainly have had behind it, and must be seen in the light of, an allusion to the outcome of actions by the British colonial masters who, at the outbreak of the Second World War, had signed a treaty with the U.S.A. in which the latter obtained several military bases in the West Indies in exchange for a number of warships, allegedly all antiquated. The result of this deal was an event of great significance in the social history of Trinidad. The Americans came in force:

> ...building airstrips and a major naval installation at the excellent deep-water harbor at Chaguaramas Bay. "The American Occupation," as this period is called in Trinidad, brought about a tremendous acceleration in the exposure of Trinidadians to the outside world. Tens of thousands of local poeple were employed in the construction and maintenance of the wartime facilities. The white American and Canadian military personnel...created something of a boom times atmosphere in the island.[8]

True to their craft, the calypsonians were not going to let this phase of Trinidad's history go by without copious comment, particularly since many of them were personally affected by both its positive and its negative aspects. For example, "Calypsonians...castigated Trinidad women for going out with the American soldiers, even when, at times, they themselves were prepared to exist off the earnings of such women."[9] In fact, a great deal of the disparaging remarks about the Trinidad female as found in the modern calypso stem directly from the reaction of the calypsonian to the fact that the Americans stole their women from right under their noses and, on leaving, abandoned the same women to the vengeance and wrath of their former lovers. Sparrow's epoch-making "Jean and Dinah" was only one in a long line of calypsoes commenting on the American presence and its effects. Sparrow sang of the revenge of the "glamour boys" who were once again going to rule Port of Spain:

> Well the girls in town feeling bad
> No more Yankees in Trinidad
> They going to close down the base for good
> Them girls have to make out how they could
> Is now they park up in town
> In for a penny, in for a pound
> Yes, is competition for so
> Trouble in town when the price drop low.

But the problem was not only in the broken male-female relationships. The influx of Americans radically changed the way of life and attitudes of many Trinidadians, for whom, for the first time, money was no problem. The Growling Tiger sought to have his fellow countrymen take stock before it was too late. He sang:

> With the circulation of money
> At the advent of the Yankee
> Take this advice from me
> Because I'm sure that after the war
> Things not going to be as they were before
> So save your money or you may be
> On the street begging charity.

Those who were enjoying this new-found wealth cared little about advice such as Tiger's and actually refused to go back to their previous way of life once the majority of the "Yankees" had left Trinidad, having down-graded the base after the war.

With the departure of the Americans, the battle between the British and the colonials was resumed. It was during this period that Atilla the Hun sang most of his political calypsoes, condemning nearly everything he felt was not in the interest of the people of Trinidad: police brutality, censorship, hypocrisy among officials, Government inefficiency etc. Of course, he was not alone in doing this. The Growling Tiger also kept up his stream of commentary and protest. His 1950 calypso "Daniel Must Go," for instance, demanded the resignation of Captain Daniel, an expatriate Education official, for reckless and drunken driving and incurred the wrath of the middle and upper classes who recoiled at the fact that one of their number could be treated in this fashion in calypso:

> The Assistant Director of Education
> He found himself in confusion
> Drunk and driving his motor car

Dangerous to the public, what behaviour!
He is a disgrace to my native land
So the public should demand his resignation

Chorus

We beg you to go, Daniel
We don't want you no more
Teacher's Union
Have a right to demand his resignation.[10]

Tiger was taken to court but the case was dismissed on a technicality.

That the calypsonian was taken to task for singing a calypso that angered the upper echelon of society was, for our purposes, of less significance than the fact that the calypsonian's role as social and political commentator was strengthened by the furore. People naturally flocked to the tent to hear the calypsonian for themselves, since there was no question of playing the offending calypso on the radio. The calypsonian understood and voiced the true feeling of the man in the street. The lower classes had their grievances, complaints and apprehensions aired through him, but, eventually, even the middle and upper classes came to identify with calypsonians like Tiger in their castigation of the ills of the Trinidad society.

It is perhaps a sign of social and political maturity among those in power that by the 1970's similar calypsoes, such as those by Chalkdust, who tackled from the Prime Minister down, were not excuses for open litigation or official reprimand. "Today, the critical calypso is accepted as a sacred part of the national tradition, and the authorities no longer dare to make any open attempt to censor them."[11] (We shall deal later in the chapter with the self-imposed censorship as practised by the radio stations.)

It is out of this background that there emerged the two significant personalities that made their indelible mark on contemporary Trinidad's social and political history: The Mighty Sparrow, who was crowned Calypso King for Carnival 1956 and later that year Dr. Eric Williams, who led his People's National Movement to victory in the elections. Both were to be immensely popular and both were to wear well, the former by his creative genius and business acumen, the latter by his overwhelming charisma that ensured continuous election victories even when the Trinidad public was openly dissatisfied with his failure to make good the many election promises and plans. Sparrow's calypsoes of social and political commentary, as well as those of fellow calypsonians, can serve to trace the major events of the Williams era and to give a very faithful indication of public sentiment on and reaction to the issues that concerned it during this same period.

* * *

The P.N.M. victory in 1956 marked the beginning of political awareness for many Trinidadians. Among the black lower and middle classes in particular, Eric Williams and his government were like a breath of fresh air. The "University of Woodford Square" had been founded in pre-election campaigning when the P.N.M. party-leader had "christened" the popular square to reflect the party's aim to educate the masses politically. Williams was idolized, as was his party. "When you ask the people what party they voting, they shouting out P.N.M.," sang the Mighty Striker, reflecting the mood of the masses that had given the P.N.M. 39% of the vote. The Mighty Sparrow, the ever-ardent P.N.M. supporter, even beneath his later criticism, saw Williams as another "William the Conqueror:"

>I am sure you've heard the story
>About Big Brain and Big Belly
>Well, Sparrow ain't fraid to talk
>Who don't like it can take a walk
>Fight finish, no bruise, no cuts
>But a man fall down on he guts
>
>Chorus
>Praise little Eric, rejoice and be glad
>We have a better future here in Trinidad
>P.N.M., it ain't got nobody like them
>For they have a champion leader
>William the Conqueror.

"Big Brain" was naturally Williams, the Doctor, and Sparrow's term showed the calypsonian's, hence the people's, admiration for the academic, for the scholar, while "Big Belly" reflected the attitude of derision with which Albert Gomes, to whom the term referred, was viewed, not without some prodding on the part of Williams. In true Trinidad "fatigue" style, Sparrow reduced the Gomes defeat to the laughable spectacle of the over-weight politician falling "on his guts." Sparrow here captured the very essence of Williams' contempt for Gomes, a contempt that is further shown a few years later when, in his *History of the People of Trinidad and Tobago,* he reduced the latter's contribution to Trinidad history to scarcely one line: "Cipriani, Butler and Solomon laboured each in his own way in the vineyard, *only to produce the barren fruit of Albert Gomes.*"[12] There is no hint in Sparrow's calypso of Gomes' intellectual achievements, for, though not in the same academic category as Williams, he had spear-headed a literary movement in the years prior to the Second World War, the importance of which is only now being fully recognized.[13] Instead, there is only the ridiculous image of the beaten politician's physical proportions: "Big Belly was with child!" It is interesting to note that Sparrow's bravado lines "Sparrow ain't fraid to talk/ Who don't like it can take a walk" would be found in essence in Williams' call a few years later to those who did not like what he was doing to "get to hell out of here," giving Sparrow the opportunity to compose one of his finest politically-oriented calypsoes. But more on that later.

The Williams government resolutely set about taking over the country's affairs from the British administrators. The struggle for Independence was on as Trinidad moved from the status of Crown Colony to that of full internal self-government. Another phase was to come when Trinidad joined the short-lived West Indian Federation, but in those initial years of the P.N.M. regime, several measures had to be adopted if the changeover of power was to mean anything. One such measure was the introduction by Williams as Minister of Finance, Planning and Development of a new income tax law. Trinidadians were going to have to pay for the promised improvements in health, education, agriculture, in fact in every area of the national budget. Sparrow sprang to Williams' defense and poured a thick coat of sugar on the bitter pill. The issue was of such interest and stirred such comment that he actually sang two "tax" calypsoes, both of which were extremely popular, with "Pay As You Earn" copping the 1958 Road March. "You Can't Get Away From the Tax" was an open exhortation to the Trinidadian to pay his taxes. Sparrow resorted to the technique of comparison, showing how the Trinidadian fares—quite well, according to Sparrow—in relation to tax-payers around the world:

> In the Virgin Isles, you got to pay taxes with a smile
> In Puerto Rico, if you don't pay, straight to jail you go
> Well, in Cuba and in Haiti, taxes higher than salary
> Don't talk about New York and Caracas
> You have to thief sometimes to pay tax.

> Chorus
> Even if your grandmother die
> You can't get away from the tax
> Don't care how you try and you try
> You can't get away from the tax
> Believe me, even if you kneel down and cry
> You can't get away from the tax
> Sparrow wouldn't tell you a lie
> You can't get away from the tax
> Scavenger or inspector
> You can't get away from the tax
> So you see, Doctor or no Doctor
> You can't get away from the tax.

Sparrow, who already saw himself as a figure of authority—"Sparrow wouldn't tell you a lie"—obviously knew all the "smart man" dodges that the Trinidadian would try in order to avoid meeting his civic responsibility: bereavement in the family, the time-worn hard luck story, rank pulling etc. None of these can work, however, since the tax is necessary, "Doctor or no Doctor."

Sparrow's first calypso dealing with taxation had shown a still loyal supporter beginning to voice the criticism of the people, though finally coming around to the same position he was to hold in the other calypso on taxation. His stand was simply that this tax was an inevitable part of political progress, something the Trinidadian had asked for when he elected the "new government." "It's a shame, it's a shame," sang Sparrow, "But we have weself to blame." His chorus went thus:

> The Doctor say to Pay As You Earn
> But Sparrow say you paying to learn
> And my father say he sharpening the axe
> For when the collector come to cut off the income tax.

So, despite all the hardships caused—"Everybody is in misery"—the tax was a necessary evil, unpalatable mainly to those "who accustom to they payroll fat." Once again, Sparrow used the threat:

> That's the law now in Trinidad
> *If you don't like it that's too bad*
> *Take your things and clear out today*
> Because all who working must pay. (My emphasis)

As a matter of fact, even the axe-sharpening father from the end of each chorus decides to sell the axe at the end and to pay his tax. One commentator has said of this calypso: "Pay As You Earn" is a classic example of the complete reversal of roles of the calypsonians, and the drastic change in the form of the calypso. The bitter, undisguised protest of Atilla and Tiger has been replaced by an evasive and complex form of criticism by Sparrow, marked by a greater poise, subtlety and irony,"[14] and Eric Williams called it "one of the best calypsos in Trinidad's history."[15]

Gradually, those who had openly defended the Doctor, those who, like Sparrow, had sung:

> Leave the damn Doctor
> And don't get me mad
> Leave the damn Doctor
> Or is murder in Trinidad

began to realize that there were problems in the society that Williams alone could not solve, though the predominantly black urban masses could not entirely escape the tendency to address themselves to the person of Williams for solutions. The Mighty Striker caught this feeling admirably when he sang:

> Annabella stocking want patching
> She want de doctah help she wid dat
> Johnson trousers falling
> He want de doctah help he wid dat
> Some want a Zephyr motor car
> Others want piece o' land
> Dorothy lose she man
> She want to complain to Doctah Williams.

Political solutions all too often meant Williams' solutions. In a way, this was understandable, since he had projected himself as a man of the people.

One has only to look at the familiar references to "Eric" or "Willie" or "the Doc" in many of the calypsoes of the day to understand to what extent a certain segment of the society did not, or refused to, see any distinction between Williams the man and Williams the head of government. It is for this reason that social commentary and political commentary in Trinidad have been so inextricably linked one with the other. Sparrow in his early commentaries, as indeed did most of his contemporaries, consistently addressed himself to, or sang about, Williams as opposed to attacking ills in general. In "No, Doctor, No," he sang:

> Listen, listen carefully
> I am a man does never be sorry
> But I went and vote for some council men
> They have me now in a pen
> After promising to give so much tender care
> They forget me as they walk out of Woodford Square
>
> Chorus
> They raise up on the taxi fare
> No, Doctor, no
> And the blasted milk gone up so dear
> No, Doctor, no
> But you must remember
> We support you in September
> You better come good
> Because I have a big piece o' mango wood.

As he had done before, Sparrow saw the humorous side of the unpleasant, namely rampant inflation. Where the father was "sharpening the axe," the calypsonian is now poised with his "mango wood," supposedly to knock sense into those who had broken their election promises. Some people were sorry "they throw down Big Belly"—a further reference to the portly Gomes—but Sparrow was prepared to "stick the pressure," even though it might kill him "in smart." How could the ruling party not like Sparrow? His immense popularity and keen sense of humour were of enormous help to it in putting and keeping in a relaxed frame of mind the Trinidad public now looking on almost helplessly as the new politics changed its way of life.

Sparrow's humorous view of events in the society attained one of its wittiest moments in his "Police Get More Pay." In 1959 the Government, on proposals from Ulric Lee, had raised the salaries of the civil servants, a popular move, to say the least, especially since it meant considerable lump-sum payments and led to a bumper back-pay Christmas. The business sector—for the most part controlled by whites and Indians—was therefore also happy at what the P.N.M. had done. Who cared about the resultant inflation? Well, according to Sparrow, the police did, for, unfortunately, the increase in salary spelt the end of corruption and bribery on the part of the public:

Them policeman mad, mad
Ah say they wild here in Trinidad
The government raise on they salary
Still they unhappy
With this raise people know they get
They don't want to pay they debts

Chorus
They use to get a shilling here, collect a shilling there
Now all of that stop
If they only say they broke, people say they making joke
They pay gone up
Ah hear the whole force in misery
No more loans and credit, you see
Ah hear they planning to lock up Lee for raising they
salary
Anytime you see they lock up Lee, is for raising they
salary.

The listener barely has time to get over Sparrow's delightfully absurd
paradox of the police arresting the very man who raised their pay before the
calypsonian launches into the description of the good life so
unceremoniously destroyed by this salary increase, so that "when you check
it together and you weigh the score/ Well they suffering worse than
before." His third stanza exposes the various ways the policemen sup-
plemented their low incomes:

They use to live cheap, cheap, cheap, cheap
And life was so sweet
Riding people taxi free
Or just walk in on the movie
You give a dance or a christening
Policeman walk in and is whisky he drinking
And know when he leaving the christening as man
You got to put something in he hand.

The final stanza ends with Sparrow's exhorting politician Mr. Lee to drive
carefully, for:

Every traffic policeman got you on his mind
And ah hear Johnson raise the fine.

Gordon Rohlehr finds these line full of comic richness and explains their
significance as follows:

A joke always loses its effect when explained, but this one
merits some analysis. Johnson is the magistrate, and, like
the policemen, on the side of the law. He has raised the
fine for traffic offences, most probably to subsidize the
same pay rise that Mr. Lee has given the policemen. But
Lee's piece of legislation has defeated its end by creating a

new misery for the people it was meant to help. The police
will therefore apprehend Mr. Lee at the first opportunity
and haul him up before Johnson, whose raised traffic fines
will at least ensure that Mr. Lee shares in some of the
misery that he has helped to create. But since Mr. Lee in
paying Johnson's fine will be subsidizing his own pay increase to policemen, he will, by the logic of the calypso, be
causing them further misery and confusion. They will
therefore have to arrest Mr. Lee again.

If one accepts the original premise of the calypso that
a policeman is naturally attuned to a system of bribery,
then all this is implied, and the listener is caught in an eter-
nal circle of absurdity.[16]

One cannot help feeling sorry for the Police, but one cannot openly condone petty bribery either, so one laughs with the calypsonian and another
matter of potential seriousness passes into the realm of Trinidad "ole talk"
and "fatigue." One notices that Sparrow does not appeal directly to
Williams, who is not mentioned in the calypso at all. Thereafter Sparrow
hardly sang about Williams, the notable exception, of course, being his
brilliant piece of political satire in 1965 when he in fact imitated the Prime
Minister throughout his "Get to Hell Outa Here." Commentary, however,
continued to show the social effects of his government's policies. Still, Sparrow referred to the Premier in 1961 as "poor Dr. Williams" in his calypso
"Present Government," which attributed the ills of the society to the lack
of a vibrant opposition:

No gas today, no phone tomorrow
What next I don't know
No drain digging, no rubbish cleaning
Only corbeaux working
The island as you see
Suffering politically
Because the present government
Have some stupid opponent
Oh Lord, man they ignorant
I say the present government
Have some stupid opponent
Not one is intelligent.

C.L.R. James, Trinidad's noted political theorist, comments on this calypso and on Sparrow's sense of the political confusion in the country at the
time: "I believe heɪe he faithfully reports public sentiment. Things are in a
mess and the reason is that the Opposition are objecting to everything."[17]
By 1979, however, a similar list of social horrors would not be imputed to
the Opposition, or lack of it, but directly to the Government, its ministers
and its "money-is-no-problem" policy which, since it came to light with the

oil bonanza, seemed to work only in fits and starts. Lord Shorty sang:

> Is five to a bed in the hospital
> And we can't hear a word from Health Minister Kamal
> Black, dirty water we have to drink
> WASA say it clean but it smelling stink
> My friend, they shouting
> Money ain't no problem
> My friend, they shouting
> Money ain't no problem

and Selwyn Ryan commented: "Shorty's beautiful and plaintive ballad 'Money Ain't No Problem' was perhaps the calypso which best reflected the mood of disenchantment with the weaknesses of the infrastructure and of the politicians and administrators who seem to be incapable of doing anything about it."[18] The noteworthy aspect of both the James and the Ryan comments is that they each point out the fidelity of the calypsonian as indicator of contemporary popular opinion.

It was clear that Eric Williams and his government were working towards one goal—the eventual and inevitable political independence of the country. This would come in 1962, during theP.N.M.'s second mandate, but not before the country experienced one more event of major political importance both for itself and for the rest of the anglophone Caribbean region as a whole. A Federal Parliament was inaugurated in Port of Spain in 1958, thus bringing together at the start of a dream the British possessions in the West Indies (with the exception of British Guiana). Sparrow, like many of the other calypsonians who praised the Federation, resorted to platitudes about regional solidarity:

> Well is big Federation for a new little nation
> On this occasion we should have a big celebration
>
> Chorus
> Whether you're a damn Trinidadian
> We all is one
> If they say you're a smart Barbadian
> We all is one
> Get away from me you greedy Grenadian
> We all is one
> I don't care if you're a bad Jamaican
> We all is one
> If you born in New York and your parents West Indian
> We all is one
> Let us join together and love one another
> We all is one.

In many ways, even Sparrow's statements on West Indian solidarity in his chorus are contradicted by his descriptions of the various islanders. These were the very attitudes that were going to turn the dream into a nightmare,

attitudes which calypsonians had long satirized. Lord Blakie, returning to a
theme already treated by Young Kitchener in 1953 in his "Experience as an
Immigration Officer" ("Good spelling and bad pronunciation/ I could hold
every Grenadian"), would later sing about the methods the police used to
stem the influx of illegal immigrants from the smaller islands "since they
hear we have Federation." They were caught by their "accent" or their
"bad English," the Trinidadian always feeling that these "small islanders
does talk bad:"

> If you see how they holding the scamps and dem
> Friends, you bound to bawl
> Some o' dem could read and spell
> But dey can't pronounce at all
> The policeman telling dem say "pig," you stupid man
> And as dey say "hag"—straight inside de van

and Grenada-born Sparrow himself had on many occasions poked fun at
the "smart Barbadians" who "pack up in this land" while in his calypso
"Yankees Back," which deals with the return of the Americans via the oil
refinery, his chorus goes:

> Fifty cents a head for Grenadians
> A dollar a head for Trinidadians
> Tobagonians free, whether big or small
> But dey say dey ain't want Barbadians at all.

These were accurate reflections of popular feeling about the outsider.
Magnified in the eyes of the politician, it was bound to lead to the complete
failure of any movement toward unity in the region. "One of the tragedies
of West Indian history," observes Glen Roach, "is the complete failure of
the Federation. . . due mainly to the insular attitude adopted by the leaders
of the three leading islands, Jamaica, Trinidad and Barbados, plus the lack
of a genuine economic base. . . Power and personal prestige meant more to
them than the benefits to be accrued from the association of islands with a
similar historical background."[19]

When the Jamaica referendum results pointed the way to that
country's leaving the Federation, Trinidad, whose ruling party "had always
stood for federation and had demanded independence for the Federation in
a period of not more than five years from its inception,"[20] nevertheless
decided to leave as well and to press for its own independence after Williams
did his now famous calculation: one from ten leaves zero. A disappointed
Sparrow sang "Federation," cited by politician and man in the street alike
as the best statement on the whole issue. C.L.R. James provides a rare first-
hand account of this calypso's impact:

> I was in the tent the night he returned and first sang it.
> When it became clear what he was saying, the audience
> froze. Trinidad had broken with the Federation. Nobody
> was saying anything and the people did not know what to

think, far less what to say. At the end of the last verse on
the first night Sparrow saw that something was wrong and
he added loudly: "I agree with the Doctor." But the people of Trinidad and Tobago only wanted a lead. Sparrow
divined their mood, for henceforth he became increasingly
bold and free. When he sang at the Savannah he put all he
had into it and the public made a great demonstration.
They wanted, how they wanted somebody to say something. He attacked Jamaica and Jamaica deserved to be attacked. But Sparrow said what people wanted to hear:
"We failed miserably."[21]

Here, in part, is what Sparrow sang, in fact winning the Calypso King Competition with this as one of his two calypsoes:

People want to know why Jamaica run
From the Federation
Yes they want to know why Jamaica run away
From the Federation
Jamaica have a right to speak she mind
That is my opinion
And if you believe in democracy
You'll agree with me

Chorus

But if they know they didn't want Federation
And they know they didn't want to unite as one
Independence was at the door
Why they didn't speak before
This is no time to say you ain't Federating no more.

Sparrow's defense of Jamaica's democratic right to "speak she mind" is
later pitted against its anger at not being granted the site of the Capital of
the Federation[22] and against its disapproval of the choice of a "Bajan
Premier." The calypsonian sees it as a shame that all those efforts should be
in vain and concludes, as C.L.R. James pointed out, that "we fail
miserably." The final stanza runs thus:

Federation boil down to simply this
Is dog eat dog and survival of the fittest
Everybody fighting for independence
Singularly, Trinidad for instance
We go get it too, so don't bother
But I find we should all be together
Not separated as we are because of Jamaica.

C.L.R. James found Sparrow's concluding lines "politically...a master-
piece." "It can mean 'I think we should all, all of us in the British West Indies, be together, and not separated as we are because Jamaica left us.' But

it could easily mean, 'I think that we who remain behind should all be together and not separated as we are because Jamaica left.'"[23] Sparrow the private citizen has said of the collapse of the Federation: "Every man wants to be a big fish in a little pond—Trinidad and all. The politicians deliberately defeated the whole aim of the Federation. . . The people were completely neglected in the entire Federation experiment. They knew nothing about each other. Yet they were to come together."[26] All the islands, therefore, had to shoulder some of the responsibility for the break-up, but, of course, Jamaica would bear the brunt of the blame for having initiated the steps leading to this state of affairs. This, nothing less, was what the average Trinidadian thought. Trinidad was seen as justified in going it alone because, as the largest of the remaining territories, it would find itself even more besieged and burdened with "small islanders," who had always flocked to Trinidad as a result of a deliberate open-door policy on the part of the British. Little did it realize that by the late 1970's its oil-based prospertiy would continue to attract them, and others, anyway.

With the Federation issue out of the way, Independence was the next step, but there were two other events that elicited comment from calypsonians prior to the crop of calypsoes dealing with the newly-acquired independence and its affects. The P.N.M. had won the 1961 elections, not without some appreciable help from the calypsonians. Williams had urged the population to vote P.N.M., with promises of "free secondary education, the emergence of the small man, responsible trade unionism, better housing and higher standards of living, improved sanitation, electricity and pipe-borne water, jobs, orderly and rational economic development."[25] The Mighty Wrangler echoed Williams' pamphleteering as he outlined the achievements of P.N.M.'s first mandate:

> Who build the schools in George Street for us?
> Nobody but the Doctor
> And the North Coast road going Las Cuevas?
> Nobody but the Doctor
> And the Housing Scheme we have in Morvant?
> Nobody but the Doctor
> And who do you think build the bridge we call the
>   Flyover?
> Nobody but the Doctor

while others made open fun of the "Mad Scientist," the popular nickname of Dr. Rudranath Capildeo, leader of the Democratic Labour Party, main opposition to the P.N.M. He was the party's answer to the Doc and had earned this name as a result of his outrageous pre-election suggestions. Sparrow's contribution was to tell his listeners not to bother with the opposition, but to get out and vote: "Wear your Balisier on Election Day." In other words, keep the P.N.M., whose party emblem is the balisier, in power.

The other event was an issue that surfaced and was solved prior to Independence Day in 1962, namely the Chaguaramas Affair, which came about as a result of negotiations leading to the start of the Federation. Chaguaramas, site of the American base, was also chosen as the site for the Federal capital, thus making it immediately imperative that it be returned to the people of Trinidad. Williams, looking beyond the Federation to Independence, resolutely set about stirring up public opinion, basing his arguments largely on the fact that the original agreement was, through some technicality, invalid. Sparrow's calypso "The Base" presented the case—pro Williams—to the people:

> So we ask the Chief Minister, he say no
> It isn't even register, it's not sealed nor stamp
> Somebody is a big, big scamp
> If they go remain, let them take the Caroni swamp.

In this, Sparrow was close to Duke, Power, Gibraltar, Cristo and others who "sang celebrating Chaguaramas, abusing the Yankee and backing the P.N.M. in the furious election of 1961."[26] The highlight of the struggle to regain possession of Chaguaramas came with the famous "March in the Rain" to the United States Consulate. Wrote Eric Williams: "When on April 22, 1960, the P.N.M. staged a demonstration in Port of Spain in which thousands marched in a steady downpour in manifestation of their support for full national independence and for the revision of the 1941 Agreement, it was quite clear that the Federal Government was doomed."[27] It was the Mighty Duke who best captured the mood of the moment:

> Well the day of all days to remember
> Was the day we marched with our Premier
> One prayer, one voice, one call
> Freedom and Independence for one and all.

This was the prevailing mood in which Trinidad and Tobago achieved independence.

An Independence Calypso Competition was, quite naturally, organized as part of the Independence celebrations. Lord Brynner won, pushing Sparrow into second place, but it was the latter's "Model Nation" that proved more popular. Brynner's effort did not really stir the people. Sparrow's did. There is usually a problem, of course, when an artist is forced to compose or create on invitation and not in response to spontaneous inspiration and it very often manifests itself in mediocrity or platitude. Though pleasant to the ear and true in part, Sparrow's calypso on independence was dripping with simplistic nationalism and chauvinism:

> The whole population of our little nation
> Is not a lot
> But oh what a mixture of races and culture
> That's what we've got

Still no major indifference
Of race, colour, religion or finance
It's amazing to you I'm sure
We didn't get independence before

How could Sparrow claim, for example, that there was no "major indifference of race" so soon after the 1961 elections when the population was split fairly and squarely on race? Was he, once again, capturing the Trinidadian's continual delusion that there is no racial problem in the society? Or was he, like his fellow calypsonians "establishing a genre of calypso which encourages Trinidadians to believe that they have a perfect society with oil, racial harmony, sugar, a stable society, a mystical lake of pitch, the most intelligent leader in the world, and steelband and Carnival the world's greatest festival, and calypso."[28] Sniper's "Portrait of Trinidad," a classic in this genre nonetheless, which won him the crown in 1965, continued where Sparrow left off in "Model Nation:"

Trinidad is my land
And of it I am proud and glad
But ah can't understand
Why some people does talk it bad.

Like Sparrow, Sniper goes on to list the many attractions of the country and its people, but Black Stalin was to do a mordant take-off on this a few years later in 1973 in his "New Portrait of Trinidad," using the same technique of listing, only this time it is the harsh reality that is presented. The Trinidad pitch lake, for example, is one of the greatest things ever seen, yet Trinidad's roads are the worst in the Caribbean! Still, the calypsonians, as mirrors of popular feeling, cannot be blamed too much for their stand on independence. They "merely represented the attitude of the people. . . [who] had emerged out of a system in which freedom and self-expression were denied them. Now that they were free, at least now that they thought they were free, they were fascinated and unrestrained in the expression of their joy."[29] The stark realities of the post-independence struggle to keep the country on its feet, the widening gap between expectation and actual output, the continued success of a party so many claimed to want out of power—except on voting day—all of these helped to maintain the calypsonian as a social and political commentator in the society.

In a way, many of Williams' policies were bearing fruit. For sure, the public was more educated about what was going on and this naturally led to its discontent whenever what it saw was not quite up to mark. Development was seen as necessary, but at what price? When, for example, the American company LockJoint was contracted to lay a sewer system in the country, the public accepted the step as necessary though expensive, but lamented the inconvenience caused. In 1964, Sparrow's "Mr. Robinson and LockJoint," in addition to commenting on the physical inconvenience of the dusty, bumpy roads, saw a side of the programme that the Government had not

shown the people, for "to know if it working we have to eat:"
>Dem big big pipe dat does carry plenty load
>Down Mucurapo Road
>Well, the only impression dat I got
>St. James people does eat a lot
>Diego Martin ain't making fun
>With some good size one
>Just like in town
>But Belmont and Laventille
>Have the smallest sewerage pipe I ever see
>
>Chorus
>The people dey got in Belmont
>Also Laventille
>Can't supply LockJoint with nothing
>In a quantity
>You see, you have to buy food
>You have to eat food
>Before LockJoint get something
>But the taxman so fierce
>The food getting scarce
>Dem pipe going to live on wind.

This is social commentary in calypso at its finest—informative, sarcastic and very witty. The calypsonian's posture is that of the bystander left to draw conclusions based solely on what he sees before him as a result of the "pulling and tugging" between LockJoint and Mr. Robinson, the Minister under whose portfolio the scheme fell; hence, large sewer pipes in the affluent neighbourhoods, smaller ones in the poorer areas. No money because of heavy taxation. No food because there is no money. "It is another deadly circle of absurdity," is the comment from Gordon Rohlehr on this superb piece of wit.[30] But Sparrow had another gem to come.

One of the members of the Cabinet and a long-time associate of the Prime Minister, Dr. Patrick Solomon, was accused of walking into a Police Station where his step-son was being detained and of personally setting him free. Large sections of the public were alarmed at Dr. Solomon's behaviour, while others thought him justified in removing his relative from the possibility of police brutality. Sparrow's "Solomon Out" showed the calypsonian torn between condoning the action of the Minister, which he does for most of the calypso, and condemning him, which he does at the end. The calypsonian is amazed that a Minister could lose his job—Solomon had resigned—on the word of a mere corporal in the Police Force. "Where in the world you could find democracy so?" Sparrow actually comes out against Solomon though he feels sympathy for him, but such is the fate of those who "acted as a Lord/Trying to spare the rod;" they "die by the sword."

The gem of political satire came as a follow-up to "Solomon Out." Sparrow's "Get to Hell Outa Here" again dealt with this celebrated affair—in fact, both calypsoes appeared on the same 1965 LP—and took its title from Williams' publicly-stated advice to those who did not like how he had handled the whole situation to do just that. On this occasion, Sparrow assumed the boastful bravado and the well-known tone of the Prime Minister. He caught the arrogant Williams as all Trinidadians, whether P.N.M. supporters or oppostion, knew him. The entire calypso deserves quotation:

> I am going to bring back Solomon
> Who don't like it, complain to the Commission
> None of them going to tell me how to run my country
> I defy any one of you to dictate for me
> I am no dictator, but when I pass an order
> Mr. Speaker, this matter must go no further
> I have nothing more to say
> And it must be done my way
> Come on, come on, come on, meeting done for the day
> This land is mine, I am the boss
> What I say goes and who vex loss
> I say that Solomon will be Minister of External Affair
> If you ain't like it, get to hell outa here
>
> I am going to do what I feel to do
> And I couldn't care less who vex or who get blue
> And if you want to test how ah strong in an election
> Leh we bet some money, ah giving odds ten to one
> I control all the money that pass through this country
> And they envy me for my African Safari
> I am politically strong, I am the weight of town
> Don't argue with me, you can't beat me in John John
> Who's not with me is my enemy
> And dust will be their destiny
> If I say that Solomon will be Minister of External Affair
> And you ain't like it, get to hell outa here
>
> Who the hell is you to jump and quarrel?
> Look, P.N.M. is mine lock, stock and barrel
> Who give you the privilege to object?
> Pay you' taxes, shut up and have respect
> I'm a tower of strength, yes
> I'm powerful but modest...unless
> I'm forced to be blunt and ruthless
> So shut up and don't squawk

> This ain't no skylark
> When I talk, no damn dog bark
> My word is law so watch you' case
> If you slip you slide, this is my place
> And I say that Solomon will be Minister of
>   External Affair
> And if you ain't like it, get to hell outa here.

The tone is harsh but the logical outcome of an attitude Sparrow himself had seen and used since his early efforts praising Williams. But after all those years, it was clear that Sparrow was disappointed with Williams' authoritarian attitude. "Indeed," says Gordon Rohlehr, "the satire is the more biting in that Sparrow uses some of the tones of the hooligan and puts them in the mouth of his protagonist. The Premier is thus reduced to the level of the badJohn.''[31] Thereafter, Sparrow's commentaries were mainly in the social vein. It was almost as if he was heeding the advice of his protagonist and leaving the strictly political field, and the P.N.M., alone. It goes without saying, however, that other calypsonians continued where Sparrow left off.

In 1966, the P.N.M. won a third mandate with 52% of the popular vote. Eric Williams still headed the party and the government. Despite everything, then, Trinidadians had returned to power the man who, according to Lord Blakie in 1965, was never where he was supposed to be when needed to solve problems:

> Ah ring Piarco terminal
> De Doctah ain't dey
> Ah ring de general hospital
> De Doctah ain't dey
> Den ah ring Royal Jail, the officer started to fret
> I am sorry, Lord Blakie, de doctah ain't reach up
>   here yet.

What this calypsonian saw was the man in the street's continuing tendency to have Williams himself solve all the country's ills. It was obvious that the model nation was having severe teething problems. Where, for instance, Sniper had sung his euphoric "Portrait of Trinidad," the Mighty Cypher, popularly known as the Clown Prince of Calypso, voiced the public's bewilderment at the fact that the Police, always very loyal to the ruling party, somehow managed not to solve the major cases while wasting time and money on minor, even absurd ones:

> Marijuana selling all over Arima
> No Police ain't see
> Superintendent sell gun for two hundred in Caroni
> No police ain't see
> A taxi leave a head in a box quite up Dabadie

> No Police ain't see
> But a deaf man say he hear Cypher cuss
> You know Police arresting me.

It was clear that all was not well and the calypsonian was right on spot to let the people have their say, a role long since abdicated by the elected representative sitting in the shadow of the authoritarian Prime Minister.

One calypsonian who saw his role as principally that of people's spokesman was the Mighty Chalkdust. He had begun singing in 1966 after composing for other calypsonians for some years, but it was in 1968 that he really came to the public's attention with his "Brain Drain." Chalkie, like Black Stalin, Valentino and Explainer in the 1970's, was part of a new generation, or rather a new spirit of social and political commentators—still in the traditional mold, but with a renewed sense of purpose. He would call names and point an accusing finger in a way Sparrow has never done and his treatment of pieces of P.N.M party and society gossip has made his calypsoes eagerly awaited and listened to every year. His melodies are not as catchy and lingering as Sparrow's, but the public willingly forgives a weak melody for biting social and political comment.

Chalkdust's entrance to the popular realm of social and political commentary was itself cloaked in controversy and his adamant stand in the face of attempted official pressure endeared him to the majority of the people, who were glad to see a non-political champion for the small man. "Brain Drain" showed the various frustrations that the local artists and scholars had to stomach, thus driving them into exile abroad. The Ministry of Education and Culture immediately saw only the strictly administrative and bureaucratic aspect of the matter, namely that a teacher in their employ was performing another job without prior permission, and one, at that, which would impair his ability to teach since it involved nightly appearances in a Calypso Tent. Chalkdust was defended by several people, including Lord Pretender, who asked why "one teacher singing foreign songs and the other can't sing we own kaiso."[32] But above all, Chalkdust defended himself. In 1969 he sang "Reply to the Ministry," in which he pointed out how several "big pappies" were making money on the side with impunity, still, says Chalkdust, echoing Cypher, "nobody ain't see:"

> Ministers and all building apartment
> And Chalkie, you and me so, can't pay the high rent
> Some work part-time in the regiment
> And get money as *Guardian* correspondent
> Civil servants for so went to Expo
> And still collecting their monthly dough
> Aubrey Adams putting on play at Queen's Hall
>   every day
> But your talent you must give away

> Gene Miles tell me: Chalkie, the Director of Culture
> Painting and selling he picture
> And it have plenty big pappy
> Cockfight and race horse bring them money
> And how come nobody ain't see?

Chalkdust used the safety of the calypso to say "to hell with the Ministry," and all those who had ever suffered as a result of its cumbersome bureaucracy naturally aligned themselves with the calypsonian, especially since everything exposed in the calypso was fairly common knowledge anyway. The Ministry, as can be guessed, failed to muzzle Chalkdust and he went on to become the foremost social and political commentator of the 1970's.

The uneasiness, disappointment and utter frustration of many of the predominantly black lower classes were given vent in 1970 in what has come to be known as the 1970 Revolution, triggered by dissension in the ranks of the Army and by various "affairs" the Government had not handled with any degree of skill, except for appointing the omnipresent Commission of Enquiry, whose reports were more often than not buried in some office. Whatever the cause, the 1970 Revolution, though relatively small on the international scale, forced Trinidadians to take a second look at themselves. Some decided that the future looked grim and left the country. Others heeded the call for national reconstruction and set about the task of rebuilding the country's image.

The 1970 Revolution came too late to be reflected in that year's calypsoes, although some commentators have observed that the 1970 crop already showed signs of the impending unrest. "There were several political calypsoes in 1970 which established the People's Parliament weeks before any marching had taken place."[33] However, the 1971 season was eagerly awaited, for the calypsonian was going to interpret events of the previous year in a way that made them intelligible to the man in the street. The calypsonians did not disappoint their followers. Several of them saw the Black Power aspect of the disturbances and commented accordingly. Both Chalkdust and Valentino addressed themselves to Dr. Williams. In "Answer to solve Black Power" Chalkdust became politician himself and put forward a comprehensive programme of possible solutions to the crisis:

> Vital areas like sugar and oil
> Must be run by sons of our soil
> Make sure that the black majority
> Fill up every hole, nook and cranny

and in "No Revolution" Valentino articulated the real reason for the marching and protests:

> We didn't want them trigger-happy police
> We only wanted to demonstrate in peace

> Yet you hold my people and charge them for sedition
> We was marching for equality
> Black unity, black dignity
> Dr. Williams, we didn't want no revolution.

In other words, the problem is one of semantics. The calypsonian obviously wants a "revolution" in the thinking of the Government whose concept of "revolution" is markedly different, since it equates the term with communism and violence.

Other calypsonians sang on the theme of national reconstruction. Stalin observed:

> If we going to rebuild the nation
> We must first think about what break it down
> We can't put it back on the same old foundation.

Words of wisdom, indeed, but who in authority was going to heed them? Sparrow's contribution was to invite all citizens to "put a hand," no doubt to help the country back on its feet. But, as usual, the public wanted to hear the calypso that came up with a slightly different angle. This came from Chalkdust.

Chalkie captured the dilemma of the 1970 unrest for the Prime Minister in his "Two Sides of a Shilling." His technique of "merely reporting some bacchanal and gossip" he had heard is used very effectively on this occasion to show former Minister A.N.R. Robinson, who, rumour had it, was planning to take control as soon as Williams had left the country on an official visit, reading to him a letter received from Williams. Chalkdust cleverly disclaims any involvement or malicious intent and the public is regaled to the "bacchanal" between the Political Leader and his one-time favourite:

> Dear A.N.R., A.N.R.
> The way you speak now I cannot believe
> You flattered me just to deceive
> You mean you waited until you see me
> Cornered with troubles and misery
> Black Power trying to eat my coo coo
> And then you throw me in the bamboo.

There follow accusation and counter-accusation, all spiked with factual details now interpreted in the mouth of the Prime Minister himself:

> I put you in charge of Finance
> You put me in a monkey pants
> I had to transfer you back
> Since my friends you attacked
> With your stupid old Finance Act.

Williams blames Robinson but the public knows better. It was clear that with that type of bickering and back-biting the small man was being sadly neglected, while the "big pappies" like Robinson were enjoying "homes in

Ellerslie Park, a big motor car, servants and chauffeur.'' For all that, Williams still emerges powerful as far as the electorate is concerned. Like Sparrow's Prime Minister in "Get to Hell Outa Here," who was "strong in an election," Chalkdust's Prime Minister also boasts of his strength at the polls:

> Ah know you waiting on election time
> But ah go open up your behind
> I will pound you like a nail.

Chalkdust, like Sparrow, captured Williams as the public had come to know him—full of vendetta and ever-ready to assign his former colleagues to oblivion. This theme was relentlessly pursued by Chalkdust throughout the rest of the 1970's. His calypsoes catalogue the plight of the fallen ones—all called by name. With each calypso Chalkdust varied the technique of reporting: not wanting to sing about the many spicy pieces of gossip he had heard about Williams and his party supporters because he "fraid Karl," the Attorney General who had piloted the Sedition Act; asking a psychiatrist attached to the Mental Asylum how he would judge anyone who, for example, sited a low-cost housing scheme in the middle of the city dump—"Somebody up in Whitehall mad," is the conclusion; receiving a call from clairvoyant Harribance Kumar warning him that "if that man put his mouth on you/Well, boy, dog eat your supper...Keep out, Chalkie, keep out/Eric Williams have goat mouth;" calling on the Prime Minister to "clear your name" in the face of the vicious rumours being noised abroad, a list of which Chalkdust naturally proceeds to enumerate; having the P.N.M. party secretary warn the General Council about the hazard of allowing Chalkdust to join the party:

> If you love him, bring him in
> But Chalkie might spoil everything;

deciding to retire from the calypso stage but "putting on his guns again" when he saw so many things going wrong in the society...

Chalkdust did not confine himself to admonishing the ruling party and in fact turned his attention to the very masses for whom he sang. Here his role was that of cultural adviser to the nation and "cultural heritage" and "identity" became frequent topics of his calypsoes. Like Eric Williams who had written in 1962:

> There can be no Mother Africa for those of African
> origin... There can be no Mother England and no dual
> loyalties... There can be no Mother China... A nation,
> like an individual, can have only one Mother. The only
> Mother we recognise is Mother Trinidad and Tobago[34]

Chalkdust called on Trinidadians of all races and cultures to recognize the fact that "culturally we are different/So that is right here you will find your identity." It is certain that Chalkie's call had a further reach among the popular masses than Williams' academic analysis at the end of his book.

Throughout the 1970's many new calypsonians chose to specialize in social and political commentary, while the older generation of Sparrow, Kitchener, Duke et al. continued to comment whenever they felt it necessary. In 1972, Sparrow's "Good Citizens" claimed that the real traitors were all high in society, the ones who control prostitution, bootlegging, dope-peddling and piracy. "Ah Digging Horrors" in 1975 outlined the many horrors Sparrow saw the man in the street facing and that same year saw Valentino singing about the paradise turned sour in "Dis Place Nice." Sparrow's query in his 1979 "Rip Off:" "Where are the leaders in whom we trust?" was echoed by nearly all the calypsonians and Explainer's answer was that they were "kicksing in Parliament," clowning while the country sank lower and lower. The oil bonanza of the mid 1970's had brought plenty of money but little relief, especially to the infrastructure. "Money is no problem," sang the Mighty Bomber, repeating Williams' famous post-oil boom statement, "but the problem is no money."

The change to Republican status in 1976 brought little change in social conditions and the calypsonians duly noted this. In fact, there are few outstanding "Republic" calypsoes, a state of affairs that emphasizes the fact that the people cared little about the official political status of the country, the very people, of course, who had seen Independence lose so much of its meaning over the years. "Same khaki pants" was the popular feeling concerning the change to Republican status.

One of the most controversial calypsoes of social and political commentary of the late 1970's was the work of Black Stalin who, quite innocently, one might add, found himself the focal point of heated dispute over his calypso "Caribbean Man." Stalin, who firmly aligns himself with the black masses, sang what could be seen as the continuation of Sparrow's "Federation," only this time the calypsonian was speaking to the West Indian politician:

> You try with a Federation, the whole thing end
>   in confusion
> Caricom and then Carifta, but somehow ah
>   smelling disaster
> Mister West Indian Politician, you went to
>   big institution
> How come you can't unite seven million?
> When a West Indian unity I know is very easy
> If you only rap to you' people and tell them like me.

But it was Stalin's chorus that caused the uproar:

> Dem is one race - De Caribbean Man
> From de same place - De Caribbean Man
> Dat make de same trip - De Caribbean Man
> On de same ship - De Caribbean Man
> So we must push one common intention

> Is for a better life in de region
> For we woman and we children
> Dat must be de ambition of de Caribbean Man
> De Caribbean Man, De Caribbean Man.

Stalin was very candid in his condemnation of those who sought solutions in empty ideologies and concluded:

> A man who don't know his history can't form no unity
> How could a man who don't know his history form his
>   own ideology
> If the rastafari movement spreading and Carifta
>   dying slow
> Den is something dem rastas on dat dem politicians
>   don't know.

Social psychologist Ramesh Deosaran, commenting on what was the title-winning composition for Stalin, claimed that the calypso was racist because it openly "pushes the view that only people of African descent are entitled to take part in Caribbean unity," and saw it as "nothing less than a gross insult to the vast number of people of other races who have come in different ships and from different places." Deosaran, himself of Indian origin, also branded the calypso as sexist because its composer displayed the attitude that Caribbean women must wait and follow.[35]

The *Trinidad Express,* to which Deosaran is a regular contributor, saw it fit to respond to this charge in its editorial under the title "We find Black Stalin not guilty:"

> We believe that Dr. Deosaran is really reading too much
> into this calypso. We must remember, in the first place,
> that a calypsonian has far wider licence than the ordinary
> person...People of African origin are by far the biggest
> ethnic group among the Caribbean peoples. And while it
> may not be ideologically correct for Stalin, in the Trinidad
> and Tobago context, to confine his comments only to
> descendants of slaves, in a regional overview it is apparent
> that he is intent on breaking down the big island-small
> island complex—one of the biggest barriers to Caricom be-
> ing a vibrant entity...
> ...it would seem to us that instead of keeping women
> down, Stalin is trying to better their lot by encouraging
> their men to give them their due.[36]

Selwyn Ryan, a colleague of Deosaran's at the St. Augustine campus and himself a special columnist for the *Express,* also defended Stalin:

> As far as the calypso itself is concerned, Stalin has ab-
> solutely nothing to apologize for. To say that the song is
> either racist or sexist is to stretch these concepts beyond
> recognition...

> One of the reasons why Blacks believe that they are
> more integrally Caribbean than any other group is that they
> alone have completely severed primordial ties with their
> "Motherland."[37]

Ryan, of African descent, also pointed out, quite correctly, that the whole
thing was really a storm in a teacup, especially since this type of calypso was
nothing new to those who followed the art form. The "racist" tone in
calypso, one might add, was not always negative, for Explainer had in "Mr.
African," for example, called upon Africans to emulate the Indians and
their solidarity and sense of purpose: "We see Indians progressing...the
Indian man he thinks differently/Every Indian for he is he family." And
long after the calypso season, at his party's annual General Convention,
Eric Williams, still in power after further election victories in 1971 and 1976
and threatening to run again in 1981, quoted lines from Stalin's calypso as
the subject of his 3½ hour address to the party. Instead of the expected
review of the state of the party or the nation, Williams gave a historical
survey of how each of the ethnic groups happened to come to the West Indies, frequently interjecting that "dem too is one race...from de same
place...dat make de same trip...on de same ship."

Stalin had touched on the very sensitive issue of race in a country
whose National Anthem boasts that "every creed and race find an equal
place." The many letters to the press proved how controversial the whole
matter turned out to be. But what was more significant in this case was the
importance the calypso, and the calypsonian, assumed in the society. The
situation recalled the 1950 controversy with the Growling Tiger when many
citizens wrote attacking the calypsonian, only in this case Stalin's views
were debated with all the seriousness befitting an academic paper. Stalin
was interviewed on radio and television and was asked questions that should
really have been put to the Caricom Secretary General. His views were taken
as the collective voice of the Caribbean blacks.

It was clear, then, that despite competition in this domain from weekly
newspapers like *The Bomb,* which naturally could comment on issues with a
rapidity unavailable to the calypsonian and which specialize in exposing
what ails the society, the calypso as social and political commentary had
come of age by the end of the 1970's and the position of the calypsonian as
the people's spokesman was well assured.

*   *   *

As can be seen, calypsoes have treated a variety of topics and subjects
as these have affected the society as a whole. It stands to reason that not
every commentary on some area of concern to the society met with approval
or was even worth considering within the confines of this study. Nearly all
the calypsoes cited in this chapter, however, were quite popular and

available on record, and ample air play by the radio stations was proof of this. These calypsoes were not only performed in the tents—thus accessible only to tent patrons—but were beamed to the entire population over long periods.

The radio stations, on directives from their Programme Directors or Boards of Directors, have for a long time practised their own brand of censorship, directed more often than not at the sexually-oriented calypso, for which one has to go to the tent. In recent times, calypsoes glorifying drug-taking were also kept off the air. Many calypsonians responded, of course, that "is de vice in dey own head," but the self-imposed ban remained all the same. Sparrow's "Jean and Dinah" was for years not played on the radio and many of his other spicy numbers have only recently been able to get past the unofficial censorship.

This action on the part of the radio stations, to be sure, only reflected the prevailing feeling among the ruling class, namely that calypsoes were somewhat sinful. "The calypsonian," notes Gordon Rohlehr, "like the old blues singer, was regarded by Christians in his society as singing devil music...Calypsonians were regarded by devout as being servants of Lucifer."[38] The Christians in control of the stations decided that during Lent, for example, sacrifices had to be made and thus for years calypsoes were not played on the air during Lent, except for a brief let up on St. Joseph's Day. One had the curious situation of calypsoes flooding the air waves up to midnight on Carnival Tuesday, only to be replaced *in toto* by other music the following morning. This absurd state of affairs caused Kitchener to sing in 1964:

> Ah go dance in de Lent
> Ah don't care who say
> Ah can't wait until Gloria Saturday.

In this respect, the newer Radio Guardian, which started operating in the late 1950's and which is now government-owned as the National Broadcasting Service, was bolder than its rival Radio Trinidad and was the first to introduce, albeit gradually, calypsoes during Lent.

This ambivalent approach to the calypso and the calypsonian has naturally not gone unnoticed by the latter and one of the frequent themes in the contemporary calypso is the lack of appreciation for the calypsonian and his cultural brother the panman. Sparrow's "Outcast" showed how:

> Calypsonians really catch hell for a long time
> To associate yourself wid dem was a big crime
> If you' sister talk to a steelband man
> De family want to break she hand
> Put she out
> Lick out every teet' in she mout'
> Pass, you outcast

and Stalin's "Pan Gone, Man Stay" told how nearly everybody benefitted from the steelband except the panman. The scant regard with which the calypsonian was viewed was no more obvious than in the early Carnival Queen shows, when the Queen, according to Sparrow, received a car for being pretty and the calypsonians received "two case o' beer" for his effort. Sparrow led the calypsonians "on-strike" for better conditions:

>The calypsonians with the talent
>Hardly getting a cent
>. . .
>So let the Queen run the show
>Without steelband and calypso
>Who want to go could go up dey
>But me ain't going no way.

Conditions have improved. The calypsonian is now being treated as a professional entertainer, but problems still persist, one of the main ones being the continued struggle by the calypsonians to have more air play on the radio during the *entire* year.

Censorship for political reasons is virtually non-existent. Even Chalkdust with his scathing attacks on the Prime Minister and his supporters has his calypsoes aired frequently. However, when least expected, the unofficial and self-imposed censorship by the radio stations rears its head. In 1979, for instance, possibly because of the title, Short Pants saw his "The Law is an Ass" refused air play. In fact, it was blanked out during the live broadcast of the semi-finals and it was only after increased pressure that it was allowed to be heard in the finals. There was nothing offensive in the calypso:

>I want to see Justice shine out in this country
>This ain't no fun, when cases are won
>We must feel that Justice is done
>Don't care how big, don't care how small
>The law must be there for all.

Failing all this, claimed Short Pants, "the law is an ass." Consequently, those who upheld the law had nothing to fear.

* * *

The calypsonian, then, in one of his roles, acts as a mirror for the society and provides the population with a voice and a platform. He also interprets that which is new, puzzling, controversial or foreign, as can be seen from the many calypsoes commenting on newsworthy world affairs, from King Edward's abdication to Princess Margaret's wedding; from the launching of the first Russian satellite to the final tumble of Skylab; from Mussolini's invasion of Ethiopia to the downfall of Idi Amin and Bokassa; from President Kennedy's blockade of Soviet ships en route to Cuba to President Nixon's resignation in disgrace over the Watergate affair...It is

clear that the views expressed fall under the general banner of popular opinion, the type the average citizen holds and discusses with his friends—views
that also include those on religion, education, drug abuse, unemployment
etc. insofar as they affect the individual and his relationship with the rest of
the society. As a result, there is no political harassment of the calypsonian
as individual, as private citizen and it is well known and accepted that the
calypsonian, too, is full of ambivalence. He can condemn in one stanza,
condone in the next and still be listened to. His role in shaping social and
political consciousness is by no means unimportant or insignificant. But, on
the whole, the calypsonian does not dabble only in social and political commentary, though some do only that; in fact he often owes his international
recognition largely to the *other* themes he treats in his calypsoes.

NOTES

[1]V.S. Naipaul, *The Middle Passage,* p. 75.

[2]Eric Williams, *History of the People of Trinidad and Tobago* (Port of Spain: P.N.M.
Publishing Company, 1962), pp. 179-180. My emphasis.

[3]Bryan Edwards, *The History, Civil and Commercial, of the British Colonies in the West
Indies,* Vol. II. London, 1819, p. 103.

[4]See Errol Hill, *The Trinidad Carnival,* p. 67.

[5]Wenzell Brown, *Angry Men, Laughing Men* (New York: Greenberg, 1947), p. 259. It is of
interest to note that the *Trinidad Guardian* commented sarcastically on Atilla's election to the
Council: "Spacious new horizons are opening for Trinidad art and culture. All we have to do is
hitch our wagon to a calypso." (*Trinidad Guardian,* 10 November 1946).

[6]Hill, p. 67.

[7]Brown, pp. 251-252.

[8]Ivor Oxaal, *Black Intellectuals Come to Power* (Cambridge, Mass: Schenkman
Publishing Company, 1968), p. 81.

[9]Gordon Rohlehr, "The Folk in Caribbean Literature," *Tapia,* 17 December 1972.

[10]*Trinidad Guardian,* 7 March 1950.

[11]Selwyn Ryan, "Voices of Protest," in *Trinidad Carnival,* No. 7 (Port of Spain: Key
Caribbean, 1979), n. pag.

[12]Williams, p. 243. My empahsis.

[13]See R. Sander (ed.), *From Trinidad* (London: Hodder & Stoughton, 1978).

[14]Glen Roach, "Calypso and Politics, 1956-1972," Unpublished Caribbean Studies
Thesis, U.W.I., St. Augustine, 1972, p. 6.

[15]Eric Williams, *Inward Hunger* (London: André Deutsch, 1969), p. 248.

[16]Gordon Rohlehr, "Sparrow as Poet," p. 91.

[17]C.L.R. James, *The Future in the Present* (London: Allison and Busby, 1977), p.193.

[18]Ryan, loc. cit.

[19]Roach, p. 9

[20]Williams, *History of the People of Trinidad and Tobago,* p. 256.

[21]C.L.R. James, loc. cit.

[22] Jamaica's Louise Bennett had captured the essence of the whole capital issue in her poem "Capital Site:"

> Dat time wen it did look sey
> De new West Indian nation
> Did want capital site more dan
> Dem wanted federation!

Louise Bennett, *Jamaica Labrish* (Jamaica: Sangster's, 1966), p. 166.

[23] C.L.R. James, p. 194.

[24] Roach, p. 12.

[25] Williams, *Inward Hunger,* p. 276.

[26] Gordon Rohlehr, "Calypso and Politics," Typescript, 1971, p. 1.

[27] Williams *History of the People of Trinidad and Tobago,* p. 276. It is a curious footnote to Trinidad's history that in the two decades since Chaguaramas has been returned to the people, rampant vandalism and government inertia have prevented the same people from enjoying to the fullest this beautiful portion of Trinidad soil.

[28] Rohlehr, "Calypso and Politics," p. 2.

[29] Roach, p. 13.

[30] Gordon Rohlehr, "Sparrow as Poet," p. 92.

[31] Gordon Rohlehr, "Sparrow and the Language of the Calypso," *Savacou,* No. 2 (September 1970), p. 98.

[32] *Trinidad Guardian,* 14 January 1969.

[33] Rohlehr, "Calypso and Politics," p. 6.

[34] Williams, *History of the People of Trinidad and Tobago,* p. 281.

[35] *Trinidad Express,* 5 March 1979, p. 1.

[36] *Trinidad Express,* 6 March 1979, p. 1.

[37] *Sunday Express,* 11 March 1979.

[38] Gordon Rohlehr, "The Development of Calypso, 1900-1940," p. 8.

SHADOW
'DE ZESS MAN'

SUGAR PLUM
Calypso

Copyright 1978
Trinity Music Publishers
5th Drive, Mount D'or Road
Champs Fleurs
Trinidad, West Indies.

Composed by Shadow
Arranger Tony Prospect

SUGAR PLUM

By Shadow

Arr. Tony Prospect

Su - gar plum, she fool - ing, Su - gar plum,

Su - gar plum, she cry - ing, Su - gar plum,

Su - gar plum, she hate me, Su - gar plum,

2nd VERSE

When, Joycie want, a next man.

My name is su-gar plum,

When, Joycie have, a weird plan,

My name is su-gar plum,

When she want man, with million,

Understand, and she see,

Me around, she will sing,

Ah sweet song.

CHORUS

4
MALE/FEMALE INTERPLAY IN THE CALYPSO

Calypsonians are mainly men of African descent, a fact that has had its bearing on the direction an overwhelming number of calypsoes have taken over the years, and this for two reasons. Firstly, slavery left its mark on the male psyche. According to Merle Hodge:

> ...the whole humiliation of slavery meant an utter devaluation of the manhood of the race; the male was powerless to carry out his traditional role of protector of the tribe, he was unable to defend either himself or his women and children from capture and transportation, from daily mishandling. His manhood was reduced to his brawn for the labor he could do for his master and to his reproductive function.[1]

The female emerged less scathed. "Caribbean woman has developed a strong moral fiber to compensate for the weakening of the male," argues this commentator, who sees as a consequence of this state of affairs "the desire of the man to do her down, to put her in her place, to safeguard his manhood threatened by the authority of the female upstart."[2] Secondly, and here we move from the wider Caribbean context to the more isolated case of Trinidad, the effect of the American presence in the island during the Second World War was, as we have seen, disastrous for the indigenous male ego. This, coupled with the devastating psychological emasculation inherent in the Crown Colony system, has played a very large part in the obsession of the Trinidad male, hence the calypsonian mirroring this attitude, with proving his manhood by either talking himself up or putting the female down.

The easiest, and thus the most frequently used area of male ego inflation is that of great sexual prowess, either natural or induced. By far the most overworked theme is that of the calypsonian's alleged insatiable sexual appetite, which causes innumerable females either to cry in ecstasy, beg for more or groan in agony if they cannot cope with their too-ardent lovers. Sparrow captured all of these reactions in his "Village Ram," an appropriate title for the stud-like role he saw himself playing:

Not a woman ever complain yet wid me
Ah ain't boasting but ah got durability

> And if a woman ever tell you that I
> Ever left her dissatisfy
> She lie, she lie, ah say she lie.

It is evident that it is of utmost importance to the calypsonian that he be
known as one who can always satisfy whatever sexual response he may have
aroused in the female, for it would, of course, be unthinkable to the male
that any apparent failure to satisfy was due to *him*. The Mighty Duke also
celebrated this stud-like approach in his "Woop, Wap Man" where he
represented the male as servicing countless females without too much
ceremony: "Woop!...Wap!...Next one!" This type of breeding-farm attitude to the choice of female partner meant that there was not much time
lost over selection. The male was quite willing to suspend his criteria for
choice for a life-long partner for the sake of the more immediate sexual
gratification. Cro Cro's calypso on "Woman, Woman" showed him openly
admitting that any woman was enough to meet his fancy, echoing in this
claim Sparrow's earlier view of himself as "Mr. Rake-and-Scrape:"

> Some men does say dey like dis one but dey don't like
>   dat one
> Dey in love today wid de thin one but dey don't like de
>   fat one
> But not me, no Siree, I cannot agree
> Because a woman is a woman for me
> Ah don't care how she ugly and obzocky

> Chorus
> I'm a busy man wid no time to lose
> Ah don't pass my hand, ah don't pick and choose
> So any kind o' woman, one foot or one hand
> Dey cannot escape from me Mr. Rake-and-Scrape.

Similarly, many of the Carnival-oriented calypsoes celebrating the two days
of revelry usually portray the calypsonian as having his eye on some female
with whom he is going to spend "las' lap" on Carnival Tuesday night in the
expected fashion. Sparrow's "Going Home Tonight" urges his female companion to:

> Have another drink again, dou dou
> Have another drink you go feel all right
> And remember we going home tonight

while Kitchener's "After Carnival" shows him enjoying his mas' with his
prospective "victim" but worrying about the weather "because if rain fall it
could stop the procedure." Indeed, many calypsoes dealing with the Carnival revelry give the distinct impression that a successful sexual encounter
is the best, if not the only way to round off the two days of bacchanal—and
this with just about any willing female.

    When natural libido fails, the calypsonian is not afraid to resort to any
of the folk aphrodisiacs known to, if not proven by, all the males in the

country—*bois bandé* and oysters in Trinidad, Pacro water in Tobago. Nothing, therefore, must prevent the calypsonian from "doing his duty," for, as Sparrow sang in 1973:

> When a woman ready and she out for blade
> And the man lay down dey he can't make the grade
> She must leave him, ah say leave him
> He ain't no kinda man at all, no kinda man at all.

"Making the grade" is seen as evidence of one's being a real man. As such, Sparrow's advice to the woman just mentioned is, naturally:

> Come, girl, enjoy yourself wid me,

for it is rare for the calypsonian ever to admit that he is unable or unwilling to "make the grade."

This constant phallic self-projection in the calypso has been compared by Gordon Rohlehr to the black American tradition of "signifying." He quotes Rap Brown's account of how it is done:

> Man you must don't know who I am. I am sweet peeter the
> womb beater, the baby maker, the cradle shaker, the deer
> slayer, the buck binder, the woman finder.[3]

The black Americans were also victims of the emasculation of slavery and life on the plantation and consequently devised a form of rhetoric to deal with this state of affairs. It gave them the psychological power and self-assertion denied them by the plantation system, since it is obvious that these were projections into fantasy as well. Still, elements of factual situations necessarily found their way into these episodes and reflected the *modus vivendi* among the blacks.

One such element found in the calypso is the attitude to paternity and fatherhood. It is to be expected that with all the alleged sexual activity the females often find themselves pregnant, upon which the sexually vigorous male usually either denies all responsibility for paternity or assumes a rather cavalier attitude to fatherhood. The frequent claim by the calypsonian is that he has been duped, that he is "minding a next man child." In other words, he is as loud in his denial as he is in boasting about his conquest before the conception. The Mighty Terror, for example, used the presence of certain racial traits to disprove paternity in his 1950 calypso "Chinese Children," claiming that since he and his Emelda were both Negro "they can't make no other kind of child but a Congo," for "when you plant corn you can't reap tannia." As a result:

> Ah fuss ah shame ah don't tell nobody
> Chinese children calling me daddy
>
> . . .
>
> I black like jet and she just like tarbaby
> Still, Chinese children calling me daddy
> Left, right, in front and behind me
> Chinese children calling me daddy.

The female is never given the credit for being able to bring off such a *tour de force* and the male, in presenting his side of the story, somehow manages to come out victorious. After all, he does come to realize what is happening, doesn't he? But he may secretly accept the fact that his mate is being supported by what may very well have been the ubiquitous Chinese shopkeeper.

Sparrow recounts a similar situation in "Child Father" where he claims that certain women run about with Tom, Dick and Harry and only find him when they are "dead out" and are already "making a baby:"

Look your daddy, girl, don't point at me
Call your daddy, child, and tell him you hungry
So much ready-made children ah getting ah so afraid
Ah don't know who is my friend or my enemy.

His attitude to his "ready-made children" was the same as Terror's to his "false children"—grudging maintenance and support all the same, probably because the presence of children is at least visible if not totally convincing proof of his manhood and also because in many instances children are treated as furniture, unceremoniously uprooted, transplanted or even "given away," farmed out to a variety of tanties and nennens. Sparrow has his "Monica Dou Dou" saying:

Sparrow ah think ah making a baby
But ah don't know who
Is de father or who to give it to,

thereby showing the casual approach to parenthood that characterized so many of these male/female relationships.

The unexpected affluence of the World War II years and those immediately following them saw the emergence of the "saga boy,"—the "glamour boy" of Sparrow's "Jean and Dinah"—always neatly dressed and much sought after by women (or, conversely, running after them). The saga boy was very often a "sweet man" as well, living off the earnings, ill-gotten or not, of his female companion and, since he was so much in demand, could ill-treat his females with impunity—and later boast about it. This attitude has persisted to the present era and naturally finds expression in the calypso. Lord Shorty in his "Sixteen Commandments" made it quite clear to his female friend that she had to follow certain rules if she wanted to keep him:

Thou shalt have no other man but me
Thou must never ask me for no money
If thou see me wid a nex' girl talking
Try and understand
Pass me straight like you ain't know me
Let me have my woman.

The Trinidad female would have found this rather "bold face" but for a long while had no voice to challenge it via the calypso, so once again the male viewpoint held sway. We shall see how the female voiced her protest later in the chapter.

The saga boy, with so many women to please, was also a "smart man," quite adept at deceiving willing females into granting certain favours, but, though he would at times resort to trickery and guile, would be upset to know that he had been outsmarted by any female. Many calypsoes show how the calypsonian wangles his way out of tricky situations by his sheer quickness of wit. A Venezuelan adventure finds Sparrow involved with a Raphaela and shows how he:

> . . . try a old trick on she
> But she was too smart for me
> When ah finish ah didn't want to pay
> But she scramble on to me before ah get away.

The recalcitrant Sparrow is threatened, in Spanish, with being shot and in fact only escapes when he wakes up "from the hospital" to which he had apparently been taken after falling ill upon eating a meal cooked by his girlfriend. This was only one of the many occasions on which the calypsonian attempted to outwit an unsuspecting female, and even when the shoe was on the other foot the entire episode is presented with the slant in favour of the crafty male, as is the case in Sparrow's "Theresa:"

> Now make up your mind, Theresa, I ain't making joke
> I don't want to use my razor, but this thing won't work
> Give me back my dollar or else settle up socially
> You could never never take my money and then making
>   old style on me.

"Making style" was all right for the male but definitely out of the question on the part of the female.

Male ego inflation, therefore, plays an important part in the calypso, but is not the only aspect of the male/female interplay, for, in addition to projecting himself as a sexual hero, the calypsonian constantly denigrates the very female partner who allows him to fulfill his sexual ambitions.

According to Merle Hodge, in Trinidad "the embarrassment of woman is part of the national ethos." This, unfortunately, is very true, particularly so among the lower-class blacks. "Young men at a loose end (usually unemployed—the devaluation of black manhood is perpetuated in economic frustration) will position themselves on a culvert, at a street corner, on a pavement, and vie with each other in the ingenuity of their comments to embarrass women going by."[4] As can be expected, this attitude spills over into the calypso and in fact "the calypsonian, the folk poet, is assured of heartfelt, howling approval when he devotes his talent to the degradation of woman."[5]

Prime among the many instances of denigration and degradation is the way calypsonians regard the physical attributes of the female. Ugliness, undoubtedly based on the Euro-centric concept of beauty, is seen as most undesirable and comments on it are frequent. In Sparrow alone one finds

Jean Marabunta: "so she ugly so she stupid;" "a ugly woman name Suzie Jumbie;" Vincentian Doreen: "so she ugly is so she repulsive"...and before him, as early as 1951, one saw the Mighty Spoiler denying these unfortunate females even the right to a "pretty" name. His "Ugly Girls with Lovely Names" had the following chorus:

> Because I see some hog-face girls name Barbara
> Some broad-faced ones name is Eleanor
> Watch some o'dem again, dey ugly as sin
> Yet their name is Patricia and Madeleine.

"Bamboleena," he argued, would be more suitable for a little girl with "picky head."

There is also frequent reference to the personal hygiene of the female. Merle Hodge's comments on this subject are illustrated by these lines:

> Clarabelle
> She could chase the Devil from Hell
> With the kind of way she does smell
> Anytime she pass yu could tell

and Sparrow's "Jean Marabunta" describes this character thus:

> This disgraceful female
> Smells like saltfish tail
> The food on she teeth like mortar
> She won't bathe, she fraid water,

a description that re-appears with respect to "Vincentian Doreen:"

> Everybody here know you fraid water
> But if you bathe you bound to smell better

while his advice to Melda, who wanted to trap him into marriage by using obeah—impossible, according to the calypsonian, since Papa Neezer, the country's most powerful obeahman, is his grandfather—is to use other ways and means to catch a husband:

> Like brushing you' teeth and bathing regular
> Soap and water keeps you fresh and clean.

In addition, in true caricature style, where the artist deliberately focuses on a weakness or deficiency and enlarges it for public scrutiny, attention is paid to whatever physical defect the female may possess, though, in all fairness to the calypsonian, this is done to all persons in the society. Still, this does not excuse the lack of gallantry as far as the female is concerned. An excellent example of this can be seen in Sparrow's "Keep the City Clean," in which he advised the municipality that its campaign to clean up the city would not be effective unless certain undesirable female elements were removed. Admittedly, Sparrow was referring to the women of easy virtue as opposed to the average female, but the overall effect was still one of denigration:

> They should hold Marabunta Jean
> And then hold picky-head Irene

And then hold stinking-mouth Doreen
If they want to keep the city clean.
Others on his list included spotty-foot Pearl, big-eye Merle, broad zip-mouth and one-breast Angela and stinking-toe Sheila. This type of listing made life unpleasant for those females who happened to have the same first names as those mentioned in the calypso[6] since the town's "limers" immediately seized the opportunity to repeat them at the appropriate time, to the extent that many girls were afraid to associate too openly with calypsonians lest, to their chagrin, they end up the subject of one of these calypsoes. Sparrow's LuLu was one such female:

Ah fraid you make a calypso on me
Ah don't want you to make no calypso on me
Ah know nobody go see and is only the two o' we
Sparrow, ah fraid you go make a calypso on me.

The females' fear of being the subject of calypsoes stemmed, without any doubt, from the fact that, more often than not, they were cast in a most unfavourable light.

The female was, for example, cast as pure sexual object, with all her intimate reactions openly revealed to ridicule:

Darling, don't bite me, don't do that, honey
I never had a man to ever do that to me
Ay ay ay ay ay dou dou darling, look me pores raise up
You making me feel weak, weak, stop, Sparrow, stop.

The over-experienced, the under-experienced, the too big, the too small, the lower class, the upper class, the old and the young, all had their experiences related in graphic detail, to the great delight of the male listeners and the bemused embarrassment of the female.

Quite naturally, the males who portrayed women in this fashion also saw only the male reaction to the female's feeble attempt at self-assertion via the choice of another companion to replace the calypsonian. Many calypsoes express the calypsonian's fear of being "horned." The Mighty Duke's 1980 "Don't Horn Me" is very explicit on this point:

Tell dem you scorn me
Darling, don't horn me
Work obeah on me
Darling, don't horn me

and female infidelity is often seen as a cause for violence:

Since ah married Dorothy
She got me going crazy
Well, is licks like fire
Ah can't take it no longer
No, No, No, ah can't take the pressure
Like she want me to commit murder

Chorus
> She have a sailor man
> She have a Chinee man
> She leggo the Chinee man
> And pick up with a policeman.

It is very possible that the cause of the infidelity is not only the female's, but the calypsonian will never admit such, infidelity being seen most times as the sole prerogative of the male, so, once again, it is the woman who is put down.

In order to give a balanced view of what the calypsonian does in the area of male/female relationships, and in all fairness to him, it must be noted that he also shows himself as the butt of female counter-reaction, with the female seen as expressing a well-appreciated sense of independence, celebrated many years ago in the internationally-famous "Matilda" who took the calypsonian's money "and run Venezuela." In a good example of the ambivalence of the calypsonian as he espouses one cause then another, Sparrow has one calypso, "Nothing for Nothing," giving the male view of the give-to-get arrangement between male and female:

> Everytime ah come to take you out you making excuse
> And every Saturday you want a dress and a new pair
>   of shoes
> Not another cent you wouldn't get until you hand up
> I'm a big big man and dis thing must stop

while another, "No Money, No Love," treats the same situation from the female's point of view:

> We can't love without money
> We can't make love on hungry belly
> Johnny, you'll be the only one I am dreaming of
> You're my turtle dove, but no money no love.

It seems, however, that the calypsonian was really willing to accept the fact that the female was in a position to reject the male's domineering attitude, one of which the calypsonian, in all honesty, is aware despite his generally anti-feminist stance. Sparrow's 13-year-old Mabel of the mid-1950's— "Don't worry you' head over me/Study for yourself not for me/Because ah young and ah strong/Ah ain't fraid no man in town"—matured into Shadow's Heartless Jane who, in the 1976 "Shift Yuh Carcass," openly defied the calypsonian:

> Bending my body, you trying to hurt me
> Shift yuh carcass, shift yuh carcass
> Your hand around my shoulder
> Like if you are the owner
> Shift yuh carcass, shift yuh carcass
> I might pelt a big stone and mash up your jawbone

You better leave me alone
Mister, drink if you drinking, dance if you dancing
Leave me let me do my thing.

The tone of violence is typical of the Mighty Shadow and not necessarily of
the reaction of most Trinidad females, though the rejection of the flirting
saga boy is encouraging, re-appearing in Sparrow's 1979 "Ah Doh Come
So" in which it is the female who takes over the role of self-projection: "If
is me you eyeing/Catch you'self you falling/No, Sparrow, No, ah do come
so." If only gradually, then, the female as represented by the male came
around to a position of fuller sexual independence, reflecting a similar state
of affairs in the society as a whole.

The female was nonetheless portrayed in favourable light in two types
of calypsoes. First of all, there was the love ballad, many of which were
close to the blues of the American blacks. The calypsonian frequently portrayed himself as a victim of "tabanca," pleading with his female to return
to him or to accept his love, lest his love-sickness drive him out of his mind.
Calypsoes of this sort were usually free of insulting remarks, though not entirely free of allusions to past sexual escapades or of threats of violence.
"Why should you leave me?" Sparrow asks his Rose, threatening "Girl,
you looking for blows." The mood is one of jilted lover, so the threat of
violence is taken in this light—the result of a mind torn apart by jealousy or
hurt. Of course, he trades on the myth that the female thrives on violence
from their suitors, a myth that has been the subject of numerous calypsoes:

Every now and then cuff them down
They'll love you long and they'll love you strong
Black up dey eye, bruise up dey knee
And they will love you eternally.

Consequently, the point of a calypso such as Sparrow's "Rose" is that the
female can feel an inner sense of flattery, triumph and pleasure over the fact
that she has had this profound effect on the male.

The second instance of favourable portrayal of the female occurs in
those calypsoes dealing with the role of mothers. Lord Kitchener had made
it plain in the early 1950's that if his mother and his wife were drowning, it
was the mother who would be saved:

Well for me I'm holding on to my mother
And my wife she'll have to excuse Kitchener
For I can always get another wife
But I can never get another mother in my life

and Mighty Destroyer's "Mother's Love" has been considered a classic in
the genre:

A mother's love we cannot forget
Wrong things we do, you bound to regret
You can have diamonds, rubies and pearls
But a mother is the greatest thing in the world.

It is somewhat ironic that the Trinidadian male should feel this way about his mother and still treat his mate (the mother or prospective mother of his own children) with such disregard and lack of respect. By way of explanation, Merle Hodge comments:

> The black man in the Caribbean is capable of deep respect for his mother and for older women in general. The worst insult in our language is to curse a man's mother. An "obscenity" flung in the heat of quarrel is, quite simply, "Yu mother!" Authority is female, a man will have instinctive qualms about disrespecting his mother or, by extension, her contemporaries, but he will take his revenge on the black female by seeking to degrade women within reach of his disrespect.[7]

Sparrow does in fact insult a contemporary of the mother in the person of the mother-in-law, but this may have been due more to the time-worn stereotype of the meddling mother-in-law than to anything else, for Sparrow, too, sings in glowing terms of his mother, feeling sorry for those who no longer have the "wealth of a mother's love." The calypsonian thus shows that he *is* capable of some feeling with regard to the female.

Relationships between males and females in which there is such a heavy emphasis on the sexual aspect naturally (but not inevitably) come around to the consideration of marriage. Here again, the calypsonian sees himself in certain set roles: being unfaithful but expecting untarnished fidelity from his spouse; being able to come and go as he pleases; not being burdened with the day-to-day problems of child rearing. And it is not beyond him to speak disparagingly of his wife as well, Sparrow referring to his as a blight in "English Society," a calypso in which an instance of wife-swapping goes awry, albeit to Sparrow's advantage, and Lord Nelson amusingly describing how his wife saves everything in their home "for company," including *herself,* while he has to make do with either inferior or make-shift replacements.

Several calypsonians offer advice on how best to maintain the marital bond, though, of course, there are many who put forward the view that formal marriage is unnecessary once the unwed partners are able to enjoy the same "privileges" as the married ones. "Why must I buy a cow," sang Sparrow, "when I know how to get milk free?" reflecting an attitude that is more wipespread than Trinidadians are willing to admit. Lord Brigo has over the years specialized in commenting on the maritial situation, from his early "Do So Ain't Like So," in which he showed males how unfair their behaviour can be, since they would not tolerate their wives doing exactly what they as husbands had done:

> She talk to George, you want to kill
> She talk to Macky you grinding still

She walk out you want to kill she wid blow
Tell dem, do so ain't like so

to his more recent "Shake up, Shake up,"—what wives must do to certain parts of their body to arouse their husbands—and his "Obey" in which both partners were exhorted to obey the restrictions imposed one on the other within the marriage. But in the final analysis, the advice that is closest to the opinion of the average Trinidad male is Lord Inventor's: "Never, never put you' mouth in husband and wife business." The peace-maker always ends up the loser.

These, then, are the main areas treated by the male calypsonians whenever they deal with male/female relationships, a decidedly favourite theme with an overwhelming number of calypsonians. They may have been on occasion relating personal experiences, though it does seem more likely and plausible that most of the episodes were fictional. However, what is of importance is the extent to which they used their material to illustrate prevailing attitudes within the Trinidad society, even when these were the result of myth and stereotype. It is of interest, therefore, to examine some of the responses of the female calypsonians, much less in number, but at least representative of the group that saw itself the target of so much of the ill-treatment and psychological denigration in the male-produced calypso.

Female calypsonians have been vastly outnumbered by their male counterparts and so have the distinct disadvantage of having to defend their sisters and daughters from a position of numerical if not of psychological weakness. By and large, there is no equivalent to the male situation, since the female calypsonians do not as a group attempt either to project themselves or to degrade their male companions. Some, like Calypso Princess, naturally fall for the same myth of sexual prowess as the males and in the calypso tent a posture such as: "I'm a hard woman to satisfy, so don't tackle me if you know you ain't able" is roundly appreciated by both males and females, while others, like Singing Diane in "You Gotta Give Away," a Lord Kitchener composition—complicating the issue, since she is then mouthing a male viewpoint dressed up as a female's—call on men to see them if they "want something." But this is not the way the majority of Trinidad females, calypsonians or not, see themselves and it is clear that this position contains a fairly large dose of that other Trinidad institution of "mamaguy."

The overall approach of the female in response to the male/female interplay is however one of support for the female in the face of male insult, misbehaviour or brutality. One of the earliest voices of female protest was that of Lady Iere, whose "Love Me or Leave Me" was very much a slogan for the oppressed women of the Caribbean as a whole and of Trinidad in particular:

You gotta love me or leave me

> Or live with Miss Dorothy
> The time is too hard
> For me to mind a man that is bad.

The use of the word "mind" seems to suggest a non-marital arrangement—not unusual—but even in such a case fidelity through love is
seen as primordial. In later years, Calypso Rose was to voice the female's
fear of being jilted, betraying along the way a touch of impatience in her advice to her beau:

> Ah don't want no engagement ring
> Ah want to hear de wedding bell ringing,

surely a stance that could put a malingering fiancé on the run.

Women's protest, reflecting the worldwide phenomenon, has in recent
times become more outspoken. In 1979, for example, Singing Francine
achieved immense popularity with her "Run Away" which advised women
to leave men who humiliated or brutalized them:

> Cat does run away, dog does run away
> Fowl does run away when you treating them bad
> What happen to you?
> Woman, you can run away too,

and in 1980, even Singing Diane continued in the same vein in "Ah Done
Wid Dat," only this time it was the offended woman expressing herself:

> Leave me, don't touch me...
> If ah don't leave now, is licks in de morning
> In de evening Ah can't take it, ah telling you flat
> Ah done wid dat.

The tent reaction to both calypsoes was the same—numerous encores as the
females showed their unrestrained appreciation of both songs. Ironically,
"Ah Done Wid Dat" was also composed by a man—arranger Ed Watson—but the sentiments were convincingly female and the performance
even more so, with the result that what remained in the public's mind was
the protest of the female in the face of male brutality.

It is clear, however, that these female voices, very articulate though
they were, are all lost eventually in the crowded arena of male performances
and that, in the long run, popular feeling will still be swayed by the male
calypsonian and his attitude both to himself and to his female companion.
The public will still enjoy the smutty calypso, reacting with what Merle
Hodge calls "howling approval" to what it feels is a piece of smut cleverly
put over. Consequently, a brief look at how some calypsonians achieve this
is in order.

The most frequent complaint against the calypso dealing with
male/female relationships has been that it is "smutty." This blanket
generalization, though true on occasion, has gone a long way toward help-
ing to deny recognition to the calypsonian. While it is certain that some
calypsonians accompany their renditions with suggestive, even downright

vulgar and lewd body movement, it is equally certain that the public will not tolerate this to any excess and will show its disapproval accordingly.

The way around outright vulgarity or open embarrassment is the use of *double entendre,* stretched to the very furthest ends of the calypsonian's fertile imagination. In its milder form, it allows the calypso to escape the self-imposed censorship of the radio stations; in its more vicious it parallels the very vulgarity or eroticism it is seeking to mask. Of this technique, novelist Earl Lovelace has said:

> The double entendre whether in politics or in such calyp-
> soes called sex was more than articulation of the slave who
> at the same time pleases his master and his peers, who must
> keep his meaning secret not because it is so multi-
> dimensional but because if he didn't he would expose
> himself. This is the case where non-opinion passes for opi-
> nion.
> ...We have learnt too well from the calypsonians that
> when we do say one thing it is safer if it appears to sound
> like another.[8]

Naturally, the situations imagined are all understandable on the basic level, though the calypsonian uses a certain range of images that the public immediately recognizes as capable of conveying the double meaning. An early Kitchener calypso shows him "climbing Mount Olga," hacking his way through overgrown grass, while in more recent times his Venezuelan Maria finally settles on particular varieties of local woods:

> The wood here in Trinidad no wood could surpass
> Ah like how it thick and hard and how it does last
> Ah try Canadian Cedar, never please me good
> But the poui and the balata, Oh Lord, dat is wood!

Sparrow relates how he went all the way to Jamaica to work for Lucy as a gardener, how he had to "water she garden" and how "in a couple months she plants start to grow." There are constant instances of adventures with cats (Sparrow's "Sell the Pussy," "Ah Fraid Pussy Bite Me," "Pussy Cat Party," "Papa Rat;" Lord Kitchener's "My Pussin," etc.) which allow the calypsonians to make continued reference to the female genitals without ap-pearing to do so directly. In some instances, the *double entendre* is really a case of dramatic irony, since the listener is made aware of a particular situa-tion of which the character in the calypso is unaware. For example, Spar-row's "Wife and Boat" tells of the calypsonian having lost his boat, his brother having lost his wife and of his commenting to an old woman who mistakenly comes to offer her sympathy to him:

> She bottom was thoroughly smash up
> She body was mark up and scratch up
>
> . . .
> Ah so glad the old lady gone.

This situation is too much for the old woman—she eventually faints—but is thoroughly amusing for the calypsonian's audience.

As can be expected, phallic symbols abound and one does not have to listen too long before hearing about "a golden sword," a "blade," a "pogo stick," a "drum stick," a "rod of correction," a "key" etc. Also frequent are images of the male "flooding" or "wetting" something belonging to the female as are images of "eating," of which Sparrow's "Congo Man" provides a classic example. He uses the commonly-held and often-caricatured situation of the African cannibal cooking the white female intruder to inform us that he "never eat a white meat yet:"

> I envy the Congo man
> Ah wish ah coulda go and shake he hand
> He eat until he stomach upset
> And I, I never eat a white meat yet.

The allusion to cannibalism serves in this instance as a convenient cover for the black West Indian male to express his desire to "prove his manhood through a fulfilled phallic vengeance for ancestral rape which proves his alienation from himself."[9] The emphasis on self-projection through phallic symbols must therefore be seen in the light of this.

Male/female encounters are thus portrayed in all manner of situations—nearly anything, in fact, that can be interpreted as a description of a sexual encounter. The following example, from Small Island Pride's 1953 "Experiences as a Taxi-driver in Venezuela," should suffice to illustrate to what lengths the calypsonian can go in his presentation of one thing as a veil for the other:

> When I start my fast driving
> Lots of funny things start happening
> The wire cross one another
> The water hose buss loose the radiator
> Well the gearbox started a grinding
> This gear so hard I can't get it to go in
> So I pull out me gear lever
> Water fly through the muffler
> And the whole car went on fire

> Chorus
> All you got to do is drive it fast
> Don't mind if she run out o' gas
> But if the radiator start to boil
> Don't stop till water overflow the coil.

In addition to the *double entendre,* the calypsonian uses obvious word play, allowing the ear, with obvious help from the calypsonian's phrasing, to complete what the eye cannot detect on paper (that is if these calypsoes were published) and to supply the real spice from the seemingly innocuous words, as in the Mightly Gypsy's "Gone for Cane" and the Lord Shorty's

"A Man for Kim." But, as is the case with any subject that appeals to man's basic instincts, there are those who object to this type of overt and semi-overt reference to what some consider most intimate or even sacred.

The radio stations are the source of calypsoes for a sizeable section of the public, quite understandably so since, even if records are bought, the output far outstrips the pocket of the average buyer. It is no doubt for this reason that the stations carefully monitor what calypsoes they play, keeping off the air any that risk offending the moral, religious or other sensibilities of the non-calypso-loving public. However, both calypsonians and calypso fans have charged that the real problem is the totally arbitrary nature of the exclusions and the slowness with which the stations come around to accepting the fact that times are indeed changing, or that what was considered indecent, lewd or suggestive (and even so, by whom?) in 1956—Sparrow's "Jean and Dinah" for instance—is not necessarily so in 1980. Furthermore, there is the charge that the same stations freely play non-calypsoes, particularly in the field of contemporary American pop music, that are equally suggestive or smutty and an accusing finger is pointed, for example, at the many songs in which the singer simulates some individual in the throes of an orgasm.

Opposition to the smutty presentation of the male/female interplay in the calypso also comes from some calypsonians themselves, both from those who, even while pleading for calypsoes to be kept "the clean way," to use the Mighty Terror's term, still delve into the *double entendre,* thereby making a distinction between open smut, linked with vulgarity and lewdness, and cleverly-veiled sexual humour, an indication of the calypsonian's skill and versatility, and from those who, like the Mighty Chalkdust, have consistently refrained from treating such subjects:

> Chalkie, it's time for you to change your style
> And sing on things that are lewd and vile
> . . .
> Eh heh? Well, my answer is simply, look here son
> Is all you blind to what going on. . .
> So understand in every land
> War is on top, the world corrupt, that's what we got
> And you want me to sing 'bout smut?
> I'd rather not.

The advent of the Black Power movement in the late 1960's and early 1970's saw the celebration of the black female by calypsonians such as Duke, Valentino and Chalkdust, who tried to inculcate a sense of pride and dignity in black womanhood in the face of constant competition from Eurocentric norms of beauty. But, in a way, the change was needed not so much in the female, who was portrayed as denying her blackness because of her use of western hair styles, cosmetics etc., but rather in the male and his approach to her, grounded as it was in psychological rejection. As such, it is encouraging to see the black female treated favourably, for "the revaluation of black womanhood inevitably also implies a restoration of black manhood."[10] Only time will tell whether the Mighty Poser's 1980 call to Trinidad men to "respect the women of the land" will be heeded and whether his fellow calypsonians, indeed even he himself, will gradually cease seeking instant popularity by projecting themselves as sexual supermen and by continuously denigrating the Trinidad female. One thing is certain, however, the calypsonian will only change when the society as a whole does. He cannot be held individually responsible for reflecting the attitude of the group that fostered him.

NOTES

[1]Merle Hodge, "The Shadow of the Whip," in Orde Coombs (ed.), *Is Massa Day Dead?* (New York: Anchor Books, 1974), p. 115.

[2]Ibid., p. 116.

[3]H.(Rap) Brown, *Die, Nigger, Die* (New York: Dial Press, 1969), p. 26.

[4]Hodge, p. 117.

[5]Ibid.

[6]One feels sorry for the many Dorothys, for example, a name particularly battered about in the calypso over the years. See Elma Reyes, "What's in a Name? Quite a lot for the Calypsonians," *Trinidad Express,* 12 October 1979, p. 17.

[7]Hodge, p. 117.

[8]Earl Lovelace, "The Beat, Sound and Soul of Calypso," *People* (Port of Spain), January 1978, p. 42.

[9]Gordon Rohlehr, "Sparrow and the Language of the Calypso," p. 85.

[10]Hodge, p. 119.

5
HUMOUR AND FANTASY IN THE CALYPSO

It is certain that the one aspect of the calypso that is universally recognized is its humour. While it is true that very serious themes are treated, the prevailing mood in such calypsoes is still clearly not one of attendant seriousness. The tent audience, for example, listens attentively to the thought-provoking calypso—be it Sparrow's "We Pass That Stage" telling Trinidadians it is time they stop their past vices and over-indulgence, Terror's "Madness" showing the horrifying effects of youths with good educations but unemployed, or Kitchener's "Housing Problem" commenting on the crisis in housing—probably shouts "kaiso" in approval and simply smiles at the fact that the calypsonian has been clever enough to draw its attention to the particular topic or to hold a point of view that either coincides with its own or that it can later tear apart in a heated "ole talk." Humour, then, is the dominant tone in most calypsoes and calypsonians more often than not look for the humorous aspect of most of their topics, a fact we have seen amply illustrated in the calyposes of social and political commentary as well as those dealing with male-female relationships on the whole.

Even where the calypsonian is acting merely as commentator on an item of interest to the populace—a great fire, a hurricane, a popular victory, a growing trend etc.—his stance is usually one of humour and he is expected to come up with something unusual or witty to satisfy the listener. The most mundane of topics can be enhanced simply by the ingenious way in which it is presented, helped along in many instances by the calypsonian's delivery. For example, when Port of Spain acquired its first sky-scraper, a modest effort by today's standards since the building had only six storeys, Sparrow saw it fit to celebrate this event with typical Trinidadian exaggeration:

Well, ah take the elevator from the ground to the top
And put on mih spying glass
Just looking around but ah had to stop and duck for the
    moon to pass
Ah try to look down but ah check back
From up dey people looking like bachack
Motor car and truck looking like toy
Cipriani self looking like a little boy.

Sparrow caught the fascination of the town folk with this new landmark:
>Trinidad coming like New York soon
>They building buildings to touch the moon

and his images of people looking like the destructive ant, of the Cipriani statue looking like that of a little boy and of his having to duck for the moon to pass provided the amusing twist that the public had come to expect.

In many instances, this amusing twist, as we have seen earlier, gives the calypso a completely different tone or meaning, and is noticeably frequent in the sexually-oriented calypso where the new twist allows the calypsonian to claim that his calypso is not really smutty at all. But it does appear in other less controversial situations, such as Sparrow's visit to Coney Island in Arima with a certain Gemma who, once on the Ferris Wheel, "wet down everybody below." Again with typical exaggeration the calypsonian shows us "people scrambling for shelter/Some with rain cloak, some with umbrella" as they try to escape this "yellow rain:"

>So never me again, Gemma, to take you any place
>Your behaviour in Arima was a shocking disgrace
>You spoil the people fete
>Rain ain't falling everybody soaking wet
>You know how shame ah feel
>You coulda do that before you went on the
>>Ferris Wheel.

Sparrow never actually says that the unfortunate young lady is having problems with her bladder, but, of course, this is what the listener believes, what he is led to believe until the last line of the last stanza when it is learned that "is a tin of orange juice she had that throw 'way!" The explanation is plausible but of little importance at this stage, the overall effect being already achieved and the damage done. In fact, the final explanation, characteristically, only serves to add to the humour of the calypso.

In addition to having an eye for the humorous in looking at actual events on which to comment, calypsonians naturally create their own hypothetical situations and treat their listeners to brief excursions into the realm of fantasy. The acknowledged master at creating these imaginative situations was the Mighty Spoiler, whose calypso career stretched from the late 1940's right up to his death in 1959. His fertile imagination conjured up situations that have passed into the domain of the classic in calypso. In "Bed Bug" Spoiler claimed that he heard that after death and burial human beings had "to come back as an insect or animal." Under the circumstances, Spoiler chose to come back as a bed bug:

>Because I'm going to bite dem young ladies, pardner
>Like a hot dog or a hamburger
>And if you know you thin, don't be in a fright
>Is only big fat women I going to bite.

Nor would he be any ordinary bed bug, opting only for people who were "quite social and respectable:"

> Such a female doctors and barristers
> Duchesses, princesses with nice figures
> And when I bite dem, friends, well I going an' boast
> And I calling myself King Bed Bug the First.

Surely, the image of the plump princess being bitten by the king of the bed bugs is extremely comical and the enduring popularity of this calypso is proof of its appeal to the population as a whole.

Spoiler's calypsoes presented a variety of situations in which the calypsonian/protagonist was on the horns of a dilemma, with the added complication of severe identity problems. He was, for example, constantly mistaken for his twin brother, even by his own wife, with the result that during a game of football it was he who was criticized off the playing field whenever his twin brother made a mistake on it, a delightfully absurd situation to be sure. But he solved the problem in the end by capitalizing on the very fact that he was often taken for his twin brother:

> We both had the flu in the hospital
> Ah play ah dead, they had a big funeral
> But they bawl like a cow when they discover
> They make a mistake and bury my twin brother.

In calypso after calypso, Spoiler presented himself as the victim of an absurdity over which he had very little control. As Mr. Everyman he was somewhat simplistic and naive, but a champion of the small man in a predicament all the same. He imagined a situation in which, in a sort of pre-women's-liberation rebellion, women learned to talk backwards, understanding nothing else and throwing all men into a state of panic:

> She wouldn't say "Johnny, where is my money?"
> She'll just bawl out "Money my is where, Johnny?"

And the back-to-front language was delivered with such rapidity by the calypsonian that it actually sounded foreign.

Spoiler's misfortunes continued at home, on All Fool's Day in particular:

> I never see more, believe in my life
> Meet a man inside my own house kissing my wife
> I ask what is that, she turn round and say
> We only fooling you, darling, is All Fool's Day

and the wife's guest is assured that "on the second of April you can't do dat." A similar situation of helplessness occurred when he took his wife to a wedding reception only to suffer the indignity of seeing the "professional" cake-sticker linger too long with her over the traditional kiss. As such, Spoiler wanted the custom of cake sticking cut out, for:

> If he kiss she on the cheek for about a half second
> I could understand. But the man
> Hugging and kissing like chewing gum stick on
> To a warm piece o' iron.

And even when he was apparently separated from his wife, he was surprised on Christmas morning to discover that Father Christmas, instead of leaving the expected goodies ("Spoiler must be hungry/Let me put a couple roast pig in dey for he") in the bag he had hung up as a replacement for the traditional but inadequately small stocking:

>...bring a police in a short pants
>With a warrant for me for wife maintenance.

Spoiler's topics were all directly inspired by and an integral part of Trinidad "ole talk," "liming" and "fatigue" sessions when friends allow their imagination to run wild as they engage in flights of fantasy and the most elaborate word play. The verbal astuteness of these fun sessions could very easily match situations such as Spoiler's being left money in a relative's will, only to find himself unable to withdraw it from the bank because "dem bigshots put theirs on mine." So, in order to get his, at one stage "two and a half feet from the top," he has to wait until the rich have taken theirs off; or Spoiler's sister being given a cat's brain while the cat received hers, with the result that the sister was all over the house "looking for mouse," while:

>The cat wey have she brain cozy on de bed
>Bussing kiss on top o' de husband head;

or the case of the only magistrate in a district being charged for speeding and having to try his own case, which he does with the help of a mirror:

>Himself told himself "You are charged for speeding"
>Himself told himself "The policeman lying"
>Himself told himself "Don't shout, this is no sport"
>And himself charge himself for contempt o' court.

The magistrate eventually fined himself twenty dollars, begged for "a li'l time to pay" and was given "five years to pay the fine."

The scenarios were hilarious, to say the least, and Spoiler went even further, imagining what would happen if a real fountain of youth were to spring up and showing beautiful young women in the midst of their "romancing" suddenly disintegrating into wrinkle-faced centurions when they forgot to renew their bath; or giving a novel slant on what life would be like in the future:

>The husband away, the wife home alone
>And they could make children on the telephone.

Spoiler's imagination was so vivid that many years after his death, calypsonians still referred to him or copied his style when they had a topic in the Spoiler vein. The Mighty Bomber's "Bomber's Dream" portrayed him as encountering the late Spoiler in a dream and being given several ideas by the latter, termed the "genius of the absurd" by critic Gordon Rohlehr:

>He turn and tell me, sing about Alice in Wonderland
>How she shed so much tears in a pitch-oil pan
>And when the pitch-oil pan overflow
>The girl swim from town to San Fernando,

and in recent times Lord Funny has obviously enjoyed the reputation of being a modern-day Spoiler, as he too explored the world of fantasy and the
absurd in the calypso. Spoiler was the calypsonian who best epitomized the
calypsonian/artist as underdog, having produced most of his work long
before the Sparrow-inspired revolution which brought recognition to the
calypsonian as entertainer, and therefore not having the full benefit of a
public that showed its appreciation in something more tangible and material
than applause, a pat on the shoulder and a quotation at the appropriate
time. Like many of the commentators who captured the mood of the society
on the social and political level, Spoiler too captured moods, moving into
areas that afforded Trinidadians an opportunity for release from their
many frustrations, for, as Gordon Rohlehr has put it:

> His peculiar contribution to the calypso form has been
> to explore the hilarious borderlands between apparent
> sense and apparent nonsense, and also to express the dry
> laughter of a bizarre age, on the edge of hope, but too
> familiar with failure and stagnation, and too directionless
> to make much effort for change.[1]

The calypsonian, then, was not only being funny; he was also providing
useful therapy for the people.

The scenarios of fantasy imagined by calypsonians have long been accepted as part and parcel of the literary output by these popular artists who
satisfy that aspect of the Trinidadian in search of the unusual along with the
humorous. Calypsoes such as Lord Kitchener's "Mango Tree" do nothing
more than allow the calypsonian the opportunity of expounding on a
hypothetical situation and the listener to be treated to a few minutes of
humour and fantasy. Kitchener wished he were a mango tree, the popular
mango *vert,* but his greatest joy would be to tantalize the youths of the
lower-class neighbourhood of Laventille by not allowing them to partake of
his fruit: "On my children they shan't eat their belly full." His chorus
showed the amusing though frustrating picture of schoolchildren lured by
the sound of what they think is ripe fruit falling only to discover otherwise:

> And look ah dropping, brip, brip, brip we go
> Brig-a-dip dem schoolchildren run below
> But when dey reach, dey hold dey head and bawl
> For when dey think is mango is my branches fall.

The entire tone of the calypso is one of revenge taken by the mango tree for
all the "stoning" to which his counterparts had been subjected by the
mischievous youngsters. Kitchener's stance is one of pure hide-and-seek
with the greedy brats and of outright sadism as he turns his "children from
ripe to green." The slant was somewhat novel. Who ever thought of looking
at the yearly bother of children noisily trying to procure mangoes from a
well-endowed tree from the tree's point of view? We are certainly here close

to the realm of the fairy tale and the later animated cartoon where the world as it is ordinarily conceived becomes all topsy-turvy. But in this case the appeal extends far beyond the usual juvenile audience at which the fairy tale and animated cartoon are aimed. It is the average adult Trinidadian who willingly listens to and appreciates the assault on his rational faculties, without there ever being the complaint that the calypsonian is pitching below his level.

Sparrow's excursions into fantasy came late in his career, mainly in the 1970's when it was clear that, having run the gamut of traditional topics, he sought to find new horizons to explore. Of course, in his many purely humorous calypsoes he had come very close to these; witness, for example, Sparrow's bewilderment at the fact that the royal Princess Margaret could marry a mere camera-man, one who "could get a good work in *Trinidad Guardian.*" Whereas "long ago in England you couldn't touch the Princess hand/Unless you real able like the Knights of the Round Table:"

> Nowadays could be any fella, you don't have to
> be muscular
> If the Princess like you, boy, you ain't have a thing
> to do
> Just take out you' camera, take a picture of her
> Tell she say cheese and if she smile
> Hold she hand and take she down the aisle.

This was indeed a big step down for royalty—from the clash of spears to the click of shutters. The pro-royalist calypsonian, a not uncommon position in the late 1950's, is obviously ill at ease in the face of the ridiculous, created, to make matters worse, as a result of the princess' prayer "to the Lord above." Here was a true situation being treated as one of fantasy because of the utter disbelief on the part of the calypsonian. In fact, Sparrow's allusion to the *Trinidad Guardian* in the very last line of the last chorus seems to suggest that Tony had better get a serious job with a newspaper and leave the princess in peace.

It is ironic that Sparrow, before himself turning to topics of fantasy, actually took a very critical look at those that were taught to young Trinidadians. In "Dan is the Man in the Van" Sparrow saw only the totally irrelevant and foreign aspect of many of the lessons in a series of popular readers—still in use today despite Sparrow's 1962 attack—and by using the very elements of the lessons to ridicule the system of learning by rote produced a masterful calypso of the absurd:

> According to the education you get when you small
> You will grow up with true ambition and respect from
> one and all
> But in my days in school they teach me like a fool
> The things they teach me I should be a
> blockheaded mule.

With this introductory stanza Sparrow set the scene for his subsequent choruses in which he juxtaposed actual situations from lessons in a series of delightful non-sequiturs that recalled Ionesco's similar process in *La Cantatrice chauve (The Bald Soprano)* where sentences of the type used by foreigners learning French were strung together into a weird avant-garde "conversation." Sparrow's final chorus went:

> Peter Peter was a pumpkin eater
> Some li'l, li'l people tie Gulliver
> When I was sick and lay abed I had two pillows at
>   my head
> The goose lay the golden egg
> Spider catch a fly
> Morocoy with wings flapping in the sky
> They beat me like a dog to learn that in school
> If me head was bright I woulda be a damn fool
> With Dan is the man in the van
> Can a pig dance a jig for a fig?
> Twirly and Twisty were two screws
> Mister Mike goes to school on a bike
> Dan is the man in the van...

That which was perfectly understandable in context was rendered ridiculous when strung together in this fashion.

Sparrows's obvious comment on the inadequacy of the material presented to the young West Indian is well taken, but the sin may have been one of excess and bad curriculum planning rather than one of simple material. "What needs to be noted here," wrote Gordon Rohlehr, "is that the poems and nursery rhymes which he attacks seem to be drawn not merely from the English tradition but from fairly wide sources. There are Aesop's fables, West Indian and African folk tales...on the whole a fairly imaginative collection."[2] There can be no quarrel, then, with the topics per se, so, to quote Rohlehr again, "satire is achieved...through a consistent caricature, distortion and mockery."[3] Sparrow took an analytical look at episodes that could not withstand such an examination, hence the resultant air of absurdity as certain elements of fantasy found themselves treated in the same manner as other elements that could withstand such scrutiny. A similar look at some of Sparrow's topics in the 1970's could easily find an observer making comments on Sparrow's material that closely resemble the latter's criticism in "Dan is the Man in the Van," and the answer to such an observation would be quite simply that some degree of fantasy, even of the absurd, acts as a sobering force in a society too concerned with problems of survival, both economic and political. But then, the average Trinidadian, with his history of response to Carnival creativity, picong and "ole talk," hardly needs such goading before entering the world of fantasy and the absurd.

In our look at the language of the calypso we saw that there are certain stock situations—the crudely shattered dream fantasy, the overheard and misinterpreted conversation—that are exploited by the calypsonian for their humorous effect. In addition to these, one finds calypsonians at times having recourse to topics that are an open invitation to stretch the credibility of the listener. A frequent ploy is the lying competition, usually played out between a Trinidadian and a native of one of the other Caribbean islands, there being the continued impression by Trinidadians that they can outwit anybody. Lord Nelson's "King Liar" (1977) recounts one such battle between a Mr. Debow, Liar the Lion and Willie Outrageous in which the name of the game is one-upmanship:

> The Outrageous say that he know a tailor
> Comes to making suit the man is a master
> If you show him a man coming round a corner
> He could make him a suit and don't even measure
> Ah talking 'bout suit sitting down correct
> Expertly made and fitting perfect
> He use to sew for Shakespeare and make suit for Hamlet
> And up to this day he ain't make a mistake yet.

Nelson knows he is in the realm of fantasy since the characters are in a lying competition, so what does it matter if Outrageous spans a few centuries to make his point? This is perfectly acceptable within the context of the Trinidadian tendency to exaggerate in his account of incidents. The response to Outrageous by Liar the Lion shows how far the imagination can be stretched, for Lion's tailor "is class:"

> Just show him the corner where the fella pass
> And he go make a suit...Dat is tailor!

Indeed. Calypsoes such as these provide a great deal of humour precisely because of the willingness on the part of the Trinidad public to be part of the game. There is absolutely no moralizing about the ill effects of telling lies—none in the calypso, none from the listener—only an appreciation of the extent to which the calypsonian succeeded in making the falsehoods memorable by their very distance from the credible.

Calypsonians also resort to personification, admittedly nothing new to the world of fables and fantasy, but used to great effect as they explore some of the same processes used by some avant-garde dramatists, for example, who, in their plays of the absurd, included in their *dramatis personae* characters such as tree, nose, phonograph etc. Both Spoiler and Sparrow had well-known Port of Spain statues take part in celebrations in the city, the former's Lord Harris going across town to "hug up Columbus" and the latter's Captain Cipriani coming down from his pedestal to "look for romance" and to "drink up and dance." The breathing of life and voice into the inanimate also allowed the calypsonian to deal with problems from a novel point of view, as was the case with Kitchener's mango tree. But whereas it was always Kitchener speaking, Sparrow, for instance, had certain months of the year voice their own protest over the fact that the 1972 Carnival was shifted to May as a result of an island-wide outbreak of poliomyelitis:

    January say "Don't ask me
    I got New Year's Day no one can take away"
    February ring C.D.C. and say
    "How the hell you could leave me and March
    And put Carnival in May?"

And in 1980 his "Rum is Macho" showed a bottle of rum using the words of the concerted advertising campaign to comment on the fact that Trinidadians were turning to its foreign counterpart whisky. The entire calypso is a plea for recognition by this product that claimed to be "as local as picong and Carnival." The Mighty Contender returned to the frequently-heard complaint that the calypso was being ignored by having the calypso itself present its case in "Think of Me," the same way Maestro had done in "Play Me" a few years earlier, while the Merchant sang about an argument among the country's newspapers, with each one naturally giving reasons why it considered itself the best informed. The calypsonians, as can be plainly seen, use a wide range of approaches as they seek to entertain and in so doing provide Trinidadians with more than their fair share of humour and fantasy.

The calypsonian as entertainer has over the years developed a personal style of presentation that is as much looked forward to as the actual calypso being sung. This, of course, restricts appreciation of this aspect to the atmosphere of the calypso tent or wherever the calypsonian is performing since its impact is visual and as such is lost on record. It is, however, appreciated as being an integral part of the oral tradition where a close rapport between performer and listener is essential. The Mighty Shadow constantly plays the role of the mysterious and satanic creature of darkness, with topics that usually complement this stance, his calypsoes being peopled with characters from Hell (Mr. Farrell in his 1974 Road March "The Bassman"), including Mr. Death himself; the Mighty Cypher comes on stage very slowly, arms raised above his head, and proceeds to explore the most humorous side of whatever topic he chooses, caring very little about the orchestra backing him but having his audience in the palm of his hand all the same; King Fighter always sings with his hat on and takes it off at the end of his performance to reveal an almost bald pate and an almost different personality as he glares at the audience while striding off the stage. It is by now an old routine for him but it still achieves the desired effect. In addition, several calypsonians resort to disguises, taking a cue from Sparrow who first did it in 1963 when he sang "Dan is the Man in the Van," appearing, quite appropriately, as a school child in uniform. The calypsonians thus introduce the element of drama into the calypso and also provide an extension of the humour therein, since the audience is often equally amused by the costume and antics of the performer.

Brief mention should here be made of a phenomenon that was seen in the mid 1970's, namely, in the performance of Rex West, the appearance of what could be termed the calypso of the absurd, the anti-calypso, akin to the anti-play or the anti-novel of the "new" dramatists and novelists. In a way, Rex West served as the embodiment and sum of all the off-beat calypsonians who had preceded him, with lyrics barely intelligible, with no recognizable melody, with no noticeable rhythm of movement and with a mediocre voice at best, even in a field in which such a voice is not necessarily a drawback. Why, then, was he so popular, with audiences clamouring for his return everywhere he performed? Was it the rarity of seeing a calypsonian of Chinese extract, who played to the Trinidadians' widely-held belief that "Chinese does dance when the music done?" The answer seems to be the same that explained the overwhelming popularity of the European theatre of the absurd of the 1950's and 1960's. The mood was right and audiences sated with the regular fare and thirsty for novelty were willing to suspend their traditional criteria for judging calypsoes and allow themselves to be literally taken for a ride not so much into fantasy, but into illogic and irrationality, thus into absurdity. But while the mood was receptive, it must be noted that other instances of the absurd in the calypso were rare, at least such as this concept was understood and practised by avant-garde dramatists—there is, for example, no deliberate use of the grotesque. Rex West, showed that Trinidadians were indeed willing to respond favourably to experiment and innovation in that which was very basic to their national art form, on condition, no doubt, that it all existed alongside the traditional and not as a total replacement of it.

It would be burdensome, even futile, to attempt to give examples of all that is humorous in the calypso, especially since some of it is quite universal in concept. Suffice it to say for the present that the calypsonian's vigilant eye perceives humour in the most serious and at times unlikely of situations, though he does not always choose to be humorous. Sparrow's "Slave," for example, is a very moving look at slavery in the new world, and with its slower tempo, is a favourite of companies specializing in modern dance, since they do interpretive steps to its music. But the same Sparrow, on two occasions, sang about the rumour that he had died and used both occasions, in "Simpson" and "Sparrow Dead," to take a humorous look at the confusion into which his friends, the women in particular, are thrown by such a bit of news:

Biscuit and coffee set, they ready to fete
The only disappointment is...I ain't dead yet.

The addition of elements of fantasy, and of the absurd, complements what is basically a situation of humour and together these elements provide many Trinidadians with a substantial portion not only of their entertainment but also of their literary fulfillment. It is fitting, therefore, that we should now look at the image of the calypsonian in the literature of his fellow Trinidadians, as well as the latter's written literary approximations of the calypso.

NOTES

[1] Gordon Rohlehr, "Sparrow as Poet," p. 87.
[2] Ibid., p. 95.
[3] Ibid., p. 96.

SHADOW

Society mad, here in Trinidad
They taking for granted, pushing me around
The world know my music is solid like brick
The people enjoy it — they jump to the beat
But when they have competition, the judges will swear
I am a comedian, so I ain' going back there
I want to catch them judges in hell
to have them jumping
just jumping, no stopping.
I want to wipe them up with some blows
And have them jumping,
just jumping, no fooling
And when I tell you jump
You have to jump, jump
And when I tell you stop
keep jumping up
And if I catch you jumping up slow
I bus' your toe.

6
THE CALYPSO IN TRINIDAD LITERATURE

Once West Indian writers started entering the mainstream of world literary output, producing works for the most part modelled on European forms—the novel in particular—it was to be expected that elements of the folk/oral tradition to which all the writers were close would be included therein. The most obvious manifestation of this has been in the domain of poetry where some of the rhythms have filtered through from the songs indigenous to the region and several commentators have pointed out the extent to which a poem like Edward Brathwaite's "Jou'vert," for example, employs the rhythm of one of these, the calypso, making it almost indispensable that the poem be read aloud to be fully appreciated. Ian McDonald's "Jaffo the Calypsonian," though clearly not using this technique, shows the calypsonian as a figure of tragi-comedy when he becomes too ill to sing for his rum-shop cronies and at the Colonial Hospital is reduced to stealing "spoons from the harried nurses to beat out rhythm on his iron bedposts."[1] The concern in this chapter, however, is principally with the novelist and the use he has made, firstly, of the calypso as a source of a grass-roots approach to life and even of a certain style of idiomatic speech and, secondly, of the calypsonian as literary personage.

It is interesting to note that it is in V.S. Naipaul's first work *Miguel Street* (though the third published in 1959) that he makes the most frequent references to the calypso. This early work is considered by many not as profound as his later ones and is in fact a series of short stories about the characters of a fictional urban street. But this setting is ideal for the presence of the calypso as the instant philosophy of the assorted band of eccentrics being observed by the boy-narrator, as well as their instant interpretation of events taking place in the society as a whole.

Very early in the work, Miguel Street achieves its own notoriety through the celebration in a popular calypso of Popo, who found himself on the wrong side of the law as a result of having "beaten up a man in Arima" because "the man had taken his wife away:"

> Nothing much happened to Popo. He had to pay a
> fine, but they let him off otherwise. The magistrate said
> that Popo had better not molest his wife again.

123

They made a calypso about Popo that was the rage
that year. It was a road march for the Carnival, and the
Andrews Sisters sang it for an American recording company:
       A certain carpenter feller went to Arima
       Looking for a mopsy called Emelda.
It was a great thing for the street.
       At school, I used to say, 'The carpenter feller was a
good friend of mine.'
       And, at cricket matches, and at the races, Hat used
to say, 'Know him? God, I used to drink with that man
night and day. Boy, he could carry his liquor.'[2]

Popo, with the obvious help of the calypso, becomes a folk hero, so much
so that when he is later jailed for having "stolen things and simply
remodelled them," the headline in the daily newspaper reads: CALYPSO
CARPENTER JAILED, and this air of hero-worship makes it possible for
the other characters to stand up for Popo, though agreeing that he has done
something foolish:

       We agreed it was a stupid thing to do. But we felt deep
       inside ourselves that Popo was really a man, perhaps a big-
       ger man than any of us. (p. 20)

Through his narrator, Naipaul constantly shows his awareness of the
role of the calypso as the "people's newspaper" or "folk archives" since
major events are recorded for posterity in it and are recalled by simple
evocation of a particular calypso at the appropriate time. When the house
of one of the characters is burnt one night, a calypso is immediately called
to mind to serve as a point of comparison:

       But what a fire it was! It was the most beautiful fire in
       Port of Spain since 1933 when the Treasury (of all places)
       burnt down, and the calypsonian sang:
       It was a glorious and beautiful scenery
       Was the burning of the Treasury, (p. 72)

and news of peace in the wake of the Second World War is associated with
the calypso that accompanied the joyous expression of relief:

       I remember the night when the news of peace reached Port
       of Spain. People just went wild and there was a carnival in
       the streets. A new calypso sprang out of nothing and
       everybody was dancing in the streets to the tune of:
       All day and all night Miss Mary Ann
       Down by the river-side she taking man, (p. 128)

while the sociological consequences of the American presence in Trinidad
are, quite naturally, seen in the light of the popular calypsoes that appeared
at that time:

       Then the war came. Hitler invaded France and the

Americans invaded Trinidad. Lord Invader made a hit
with his calypso:

> I was living with my decent and contented wife
> Until the soliders came and broke up my life.

For the first time in Trinidad there was work for
everybody, and the Americans paid well. Invader sang:

> Father, mother and daughter
> Working for the Yankee dollar!
> Money in the land!
> The Yankee dollar, oh! (p. 143)

This familiarity with the calypso and its role in the society is, however, not
confined to the narrator alone, since many of the other characters use
quotations from popular calypsoes to round off arguments, encapsulate
personal bits of philosophy or substantiate certain stereotyped attitudes.

In the world of Miguel Street, where what is objected to, at least on the
surface, by the rest of the "respectable" society as a whole is considered
perfectly normal by the majority of the characters, one finds many of the
attitudes prevalent in calypsoes dealing with male-female relationships also
prevalent among the street's dwellers. Of Nathaniel, Laura's new man, ap-
pearing in her life rather belatedly, since she already has six children by six
different fathers before he makes his contribution, the narrator says:

> Nathaniel, in the early stages, tried to make us believe
> that he knew how to keep Laura in her place. He hinted
> that he used to beat her. He used to say, "Woman and
> them like a good dose of blows, you know. You know the
> calypso:
>
> > Every now and then just knock them down.
> > Every now and then just throw them down.
> > Black up their eye and bruise up their knee
> > And then they love you eternally.
> > Is gospel truth about woman.' (p. 87)

Nathaniel would have everyone believe that he follows the stereotype, only,
unfortunately, he "was lying of course. It wasn't he who was giving the
blows, it was Laura," which forces another street character, Eddoes, to
conclude: "It look like they make up that calypso about men, not women."
(p. 87) This ironic twist is itself worthy of a calypso.

Eddoes too has his brand of problems which are explained with the
help of a calypso, for when his girl is "making baby," Hat tries to make
him see the potential guile of many girls in such a situation:

> Hat said, 'The calypsonian was right, you hear.
> > Man centipede bad.
> > Woman centipede more than bad.' (p. 98)

As it turns out, Eddoes does seem to have been stung by the "woman cen-
tipede:"

> ...one glance at Pleasure made us know that she
> couldn't be Eddoes's baby.
>   Boyee began whistling the calypso:
>   Chinese children calling me Daddy!
>   I black like jet
>   My wife like tar-baby
>   And still—
>   Chinese children calling me Daddy!
>   Oh God, somebody putting milk in my coffee. (p. 99)

One notices that the immediate reaction to the "false child"—to use the
Mighty Terror's term in the actual calypso—is to place the entire situation
in the context of a well-known calypso, and that in the other instances when
a calypso is introduced as the culmination of an argument or discussion, we
are told that the calypsonian "was right" or that what he had sung was
"gospel truth." It is obvious, then, that the calypso is fundamental to the
lives of these characters and that, further, it is seen as a sort of poor man's
philosophy, making it possible for the eccentrics of this urban slum to come
to terms with themselves and with those around them.

Speaking about Samuel Selvon, critic Kenneth Ramchand has said that
it is in his works that "the language of the implied author boldly declares
itself as dialect differing little from the language of the characters," and he
goes on to point out that in the story "Brackley and the Bed," for example,
Selvon "takes up the stance of the calypsonian...closing the gap between
the language of narration and the language of the fictional character."[3]
There can be no doubt that of the major West Indian novelists it is Selvon
who is the most successful at observing the realities of life around him with
the same eyes as the calypsonian, and he is seen by Gordon Rohlehr as
"relating to the same tradition of style and rhetoric which produced calypsonians like the legendary Spoiler, Wonder, Panther, Melody, Lion, Tiger,
Invader, Atilla, Kitchener, Beginner and Dictator, all figures of the
forties,"[4] and by Michel Fabre as using in his fiction a "calypso style" in
which "the calypso...represents a return to authentic popular sources. At
the same time, it creates a mood of relaxation which facilitates the sharing
of non-verbalized assumptions between narrator and reader."[5] An excellent
example of this can be seen in the comparison of the following passages, the
first from Selvon's *A Brighter Sun* and the second from the Mighty Panther's calypso "Taxi Drivers," in both of which the dog-eat-dog hustling of
the taxi drivers in search of their daily bread is the subject of ridicule:[6]

> Boysie turned to Tiger. "Boy, dese taximen does have
> tings their own way too much. Some of dem does tell yuh
> dey leaving right away, and wen yuh get in de car, is
> because they making rounds all Charlotte Street for more
> passengers, and wat yuh cud do? Nothing, because yuh in

de car already. As for wen dey going down south! Boy, dat
is trouble self. All dem touts by de railway station, from de
time dey see yuh wid a grip in yuh hand, dey start hustling.
'South, mister? Yuh going south? Look ah nice car
here—it have radio. Leaving right away. South direct.'
And dis time de smart driver have bout three tout sitting
down quiet as if dey is passengers.[7]

There are obvious similarities between Selvon's lines and Panther's calypso:

You may be standing on any pavement
Asking someone questions on the government
All you see is taxis in a line
And all you do is answering questions all the time...

Chorus

An is PeeeeP...One to go
You shake your head, you tell them no
Braaw...they blow again
You shake your head, you tell them no again
And is, San Juan, Tunapuna, Arima, Sangre
Grande...Madam,
you going? I am de fellar who give you a lift in Toco
last week...You can't remember me?
And they pointing their finger all over the place
Somebody have a right to spit in their face,

and at one stage, over the music, the calypsonian comes in with an even
closer imitation of the hustling taxi driver:

He say, 'Panther, you're a old calypsonian I know a
long time. You mean to say when I want to go to
Carenage you won't go wid me? Whe it is at all?
Anywhere you going ah carrying you, Diego Martin,
Four Road, Tamana, Bucco Point, Uphill...any way at
all..

The similarity of language is striking, showing to what extent both the
novelist and the calypsonian have an ear for the language of the people.

The logical extension of this closeness to the language of the people is
found in *The Lonely Londoners*, where the entire novel is written in
Trinidad creole, a language that is filled with all the elements of "ole talk,"
"heckling," "fatigue," "picong" and "mamaguy," as opposed to, say, *A
Brighter Sun* where this, though used in the direct speech of the characters,
gives way to standard English for the narrative. The work could easily be
termed a "calypso novel," since so many of the techniques of the calypso
are incorporated into its language, so many of the characters seem to step
right out of well-known calypsoes—there is even a Sir Galahad, a perfect
calypso sobriquet—so many of the episodes read like little calypsoes in prose:

Galahad laugh. 'Yes, I know. You ever hear bout the
time when Brackley sleep with a whore?''
'No.'
'It was Tina. It was a Tuesday night, so things was
really bad with the girls, and Brackley broach Tina. She
say all right, but only thing Brackley must get up early in
the morning and out off, because she don't want them
other girls to know she sleep with a fellar like him.
Brackley agree, and Tina carry him home in George Street
and they went to sleep. Next morning Tina get up very early and gone in the market for her fresh piece of beef, thinking that by the time she come back Brackley would be
gone. But Brackley take time and get up, and start to yawn
and stretch, and he open the window and stand up there
scratching his chest. All them whores in the backyard looking at Brackley and saying: "A-a! Brackley sleep with
Tina, me child!" And Brackley stand up there waving his
hand: "Morning, neighbour! morning!" and laughing all
over his face. When Tina come back she start to kick up
hell, but Brackley say, "What the hell happen to you? I
give you my money and I sleep with you and everybody
know."''[8]

This same procedure can be found in the London section of *Ways of
Sunlight,* where Selvon actually refers to his "Brackley and the Bed" as a
"ballad." The following passage also has many of the elements of the style
of the calypso—humour, surprise etc.:

Brackley hail from Tobago, which part they have it to
say Robinson Crusoe used to hang out with Man Friday.
Things was brown in that island and he make for England
and manage to get a work and was just settling down when
bam! he get a letter from his aunt saying that Teena want
to come England too.
Teena was Brackley distant cousin and they was good
friends in Tobago. In fact, the other reason why Brackley
hustle from the island is because it did look like he and
Teena was heading for a little married thing, and Brackley
run.
Well, right away he write aunty and say no, no,
because he have a feeling this girl would make botheration
if she come England. The aunt write back to say she didn't
mean to say that Teena want to come England, but that
Teena left Tobago for England already.
Brackley hold his head and bawl.[9]

The point being made, of course, is not that Selvon is a calypsonian, but simply that he, very much like the calypsonian, captures the essence of the speech patterns and thoughts of the average Trinidadian, relating as they both do in this instance to the vibrant oral tradition.

The character of the calypsonian also appears in the novels and short stories of the Trinidad writers, a most plausible and expected occurrence in the light of the types that people many of these works. In his B. Wordsworth, one of the *Miguel Street* characters. Naipaul has a poet *manqué* who sings calypsoes:

> 'How you does live, Mr. Wordsworth?' I asked him
> one day.
> He said, 'You mean how I get money?'
> When I nodded, he laughed in a crooked way.
> He said, 'I sing calyposes in the calypso season.'
> 'And that last you the rest of the year?'
> 'It is enough.' (pp. 50-51)

He never discloses what he sings or how much money is "enough" but it is not too difficult to guess that the financial gain was relatively small. In fact, the mysterious Mr. Wordsworth simply disappeared. "It was as though B. Wordsworth had never existed." (p. 52)

Selvon's "Calypso in London," one of the stories from *Ways of Sunlight,* shows a calypsonian in exile, having gone to the "mother country" after achieving a fair degree of success at home:

> Sometimes Hotboy in some real oldtalk about them days
> back home, telling Rahamut about how he was one of the
> best calypsonians it had in Trinidad, how he compose
> numbers like 'I Saw You Doing It Last Night' and 'That Is
> A Thing I Could Do Anytime, Anywhere.' Well Hotboy
> always saying about how he would make a comeback one
> day, how he would compose a calypso that would be
> hearts, and it would sell plenty and he would make money
> and come rich. (pp. 126-127)

But it is Hotboy's friend Mangohead who is shown in the creative mood, with the former calypsonian, the "real" one, acting as critic:

> Mangohead suddenly feeling creative. As if all the troubles
> he in put him in a thoughtful mood, and while he
> meditating on the downs of life, he feel like composing a
> calypso that would tell everybody how life treating him.
>> It had a time in this country
>> When everybody happy excepting me
>> I can't get a work no matter how I try
>> It look as if hard times riding me high. (p. 127)

The lyrics show some promise, but Mangohead needs Hotboy's help to "set up a tune for them"—good melody off-setting weak lyric as usual. As it turns out, Mangohead has always used Hotboy to judge his compositions: "Hot tired asking the Mango to leave calypso alone, telling him this is not his line... But Mango, who tell you you could write calypso?" (p. 128) The criticism however leads to the creation of what the original calypsonian considers acceptable:

'You think we still in Trinidad? This is London, man, this is London. The people want calypso on topical subject.'

'That is only the first verse,' Mango say, 'I am coming to the Suez issue.'

And Mango, as if he get an inspiration, start to extemporise on Nasser and Eden and how he will give them the dope—the best thing is to pass the ships round the Cape of Good Hope.

'Like you have something there,' Hotboy concede, and he begin to hum a little tune.

Well in fifteen minutes time, in that tailor shop in the East End, the two boys had a calypso shaping up, and it wasn't a bad number either. (pp. 128-129)

The creative process is noteworthy, since many calypsonians have acknowledged this type of situation to be the genesis of many of their songs, and even the composition of Sparrow's classic "Jean and Dinah" has been the subject of controversy among calypso aficionados. What is also true, unfortunately, is the outcome of the whole process. Hotboy appropriates the calypso lyrics and has dreams of a "comeback:" "He could hear this calypso playing all about in London, and people going wild when they hear it." (p. 129) Mangohead used his breakthrough only as an opportunity to "tap" Hotboy for a small loan and Hotboy claims in the end that "he sell the calypso:"

But up to now I can't hear it playing or singing anywhere, though I sure the number was really hearts, and would make some money for the boys if it catch on and sell. (p. 131)

Selvons' calypsonian, then, drawn in the quick strokes of the caricaturist, is easily recognizable to those who are aware of the frustration and exploitation that too many calypsonians have experienced over the years. The situation of the 1950's as portrayed in Selvon's story has remained painfully real for a great number of calypsonians—fleeting popularity followed by years of mediocrity or oblivion.

Rather interestingly, Selvon has another short story called "Calypsonian"[10] which is set in Trinidad and which reads like a re-working of "Calypso in London" for a Trinidad audience, though, in the absence of any definitive indication from Selvon, the opposite is also quite possible.

"Calypsonian" is longer and has a slightly different orientation from "Calypso in London," but the similarities are nonetheless very striking, leading one to conclude that one story is obviously an edited version of the other. A couple of examples should serve to illustrate this:

Razor Blade's composition shows only cosmetic changes from the one we saw done by Mangohead:

It had a time in this colony
When everybody have money excepting me
I can't get a work no matter how I try
It look as if good times pass me by (pp. 76-77)

and the reaction to the composition of a new calypso is described in "Calypso in London" as follows:

Well in fifteen minutes time, in that tailor shop in the East End, the two boys had a calypso shaping up, and it wasn't a bad number, either.

Rahamut and the English Assistant he have come and stand up listening, and when the calypso finish singing the English fellar say: 'That is one of the best calypsos I ever heard.'

But Rahamut say: 'Why you don't shut your mouth? What you English people know about calypso?' (p. 129)

while in "Calypsonian" Selvon writes:

They begin to work on the song, and One Foot so good that in two twos he fix up a tune. . .

Well, Rahamut and the other Indian fellar who does help him out with the sewing come up and listen.

"What you think of this new number, papa?" the Blade ask Rahamut.

Rahamut scratch his head and say: "Let me get that tune again."

So they begin again, beating on the table and the bottle. . .

When they finished the fellar who does help Rahamut say: "That is hearts."

But Rahamut say: "Why you don't shut your mouth? What all-you Indian know about calypso?" (p.79)

For all the interest of the comparison of the textual similarities, however, what is more significant for our purposes is the image Selvon provides of the calypsonian at home among his own countrymen, an image which completes, or is completed by, the one of him in exile.

Razor Blade, the calypsonian at home, suffers from the seasonal nature of the calypso—and no doubt also from the fact that he has no other marketable skills. He is kept from utter despair by the thought that the approaching calypso season will bring certain financial ease. "Wait until the

calypso season start," he keeps repeating, "I go be reaping a harvest." One
notes his self-assurance but, unfortunately, his cavalier attitude to the
management of his earnings usually leaves him no better off once the season
is over. Razor Blade falls prey to the popular calypsonian stereotype of fancy dresser: "Razor Blade remembered how last year he was sitting
pretty—two-tone Technic, gaberdeen suit, hot tie" (p. 73); of big spender:
"He begin to think again about the last calypso season, when he was
holding big, and uses to go up by the high-class Chinee restaurant in St.
Vincent Street" (p. 74); and of life-of-the-party: "He remember how them
waitresses used to hustle to serve him, and one night the talk get around that
Razor Blade, the Calypsonian, was in the place, and they insist that he give
them a number" (p. 74).

Razor Blade is aware of the frustration of being a calypsonian at this
point in time. He remembers the way one particular calypsonian was exploited by "an American fellar" who got the Andrews Sisters to sing his
calypso, but he sees only the financial aspect of the eventual court settlement of the copyright issue and therefore dreams of a similar means of
escape and recognition:

> ...whenever he write a calypso, he always praying that
> some big-shot from America would hear it and like it, and
> want to set it up good. The Blade uses to go in Frederick
> Street and Marine Square by the one-two music shops, and
> look at all the popular songs, set up in notes and words,
> with the name of the fellar who write it big on the front,
> and sometimes his photograph too. And Razor Blade uses
> to think: "But why I can't write song like that too, and
> have my name all over the place?" (p. 75)

He is also aware of the low esteem in which the calypso and calypsonian are
held:

> ...he...tell the clerks and them that he does write calyp-
> sos. But they only laugh at him, because they does think
> that calypso is no song at all, that what is song is numbers
> like 'I've Got You Under My Skin' and 'Sentimental
> Journey,' what *real* American composers write. (pp. 75-76.
> My emphasis.)

and is later reminded by his calypsonian friend One Foot that "Us calypsonians have to keep we dignity" (p. 81).

It is for these reasons that it is so pathetic to see Razor Blade fail. He
fails because he does not have the strength and patience needed to withstand
the despair of the post-calypso-season period when he is "catching his
royal, and can't get a work noway." And so he rationalizes that "it don't
take plenty to make a t'ief;" only, it is difficult to stop once one has started,
and the final scene of the story shows Razor Blade, to his horror, bungling
what had originally looked like an easy robbery attempt, and a petty one at

that, and almost freezing in his tracks as he is chased and gasps: "Oh God! Oh God!"

For all its humour, then, "Calypsonian" leaves a bitter taste in the mouth and can hardly be considered flattering to the genuine calypsonian because of the twist the story takes. The frustration, the creative effort, the hustler attitude all ring true, as they do in "Calypso in London." However, while it is one thing to be recognized as a "smart man," it is a totally different matter to be openly involved in crime, no matter how petty, no matter how accidental. From the calypsonian's point of view, what is unfortunate about "Calypsonian" is that a significant section of the Trinidad public has over the years, justifiably or not, believed that this is precisely the type of life led by the majority of calypsonians.

By far the fullest treatment of the calypsonian in the contemporary Trinidadian novel is Earl Lovelace's in *The Dragon Can't Dance*. We see Philo—his sobriquet is never given—as he moves up from the urban slum hill, where he would do anything to conquer the mulatto yard "queen," Miss Cleothilda, to success—women, car, house in suburban residential neighbourhood etc.—and back to the woman he always wanted, if not to the yard where she lived. Lovelace's success in the portrayal of the calypsonian lies in his thorough understanding of what motivates this character, in his understanding of the calypsonian as folk philosopher, even in his calypso compositions which ring true—one almost hears them already set to music.

Philo's rise to fame comes as a result of a calypso which, in typical fashion, uses the *double entendre* to project the calypsonian as sexually prolific:

> I am the axe man cutting forests down
> I am the axe man working all over town
> If you have a tree to cut, I am the man to call
> I never put my axe on a tree and it didn't break and
>   fall.[11]

Lovelace himself comments on the "Axe Man:"

> It was one of those suggestive calypsos—filled with
> phallic symbolism and sexual overtones—was, rather, a
> simple metaphor of male sexual conquest, and when Philo
> sang it in the tent later that very evening he would get three
> encores for it. And patrons in the front seat would throw
> dollar bills on to the stage. (p. 112)

Philo is however aware that the "smutty" calypso represents a departure from his normal style, but, like Chalkdust, he is "aware that up there is sex bare they want to hear." Unlike Chalkdust, though, he switches his style with an eye on the "crown:"

'I know you must be saying that I change, that this is not
my style, my kinda song, that I ain't protesting again, I
ain't singing against the bad things in the place. But, man,
you have to sing what the people want to hear.'
. . .
'Man, year in year out, I singing about how people hungry,
how officials ain't doing their duty, and what I get, man?
What I get? I want to win the Calypso King crown, at least
reach the finals this year, one year, so I could say after this
whole thing finish, "I was there".' (pp. 112-113)

And like the drunkard who never admits he is drunk, Philo blinds himself to
the fact that impatience has him already selling his artist integrity for the
silver of instant celebrity. "It was," comments the narrator, "like
everybody, people, felt they were running out of time, and they had to have
something to show for being here." (p. 113)

Philo's success is symbolized by two outward signs. The first is his new
style of clothing, falling as he does for the stereotype of the gaudily-dressed
calypsonian—silk shirts, bright scarves, white panama hat with long, colourful feathers—and even when this very success alienates him from his
former buddies, Philo continues to decorate himself in these colourful trim-
mings, "as if he wanted to hide himself, to make himself appear so cosquel*
that any fool would know that he had to be found elsewhere, apart from the
costume, within it." (p. 155) The second is his easier access to Miss
Cleothilda, as is evidenced by his being allowed to ascend her steps and to
sit down on her verandah, all set to penetrate her bedroom, which yard
gossip has him doing even before it actually happens: "You can't know how
far he go when the night come."' In the end, this latter symbol of success is
also a symbol of Philo's being absorbed by what critic Victor Questel has
termed "the system."[12]

The calypsoes produced by Philo are, for the most part, similar to real
ones heard by the Trinidad public over the years. There are echoes of the
Mighty Shadow's "Winston" in Philo's:

Since I know myself people beating me
I asking them why, they wouldn't tell me
At last I know why, is because I don't cry
Bobolee don't have water in their eye. (p. 228)

His "Women Running Me Down" continues the image of the axe-man and
is a sort of antidote to Sparrow's "Mr. Rake-and-Scrape." His "Hooligans
in Port of Spain" sounds like a combination of Sparrow's "Royal Jail" and
"Hangman Cemetery:"

Hooligans in Port of Spain messing up the place
Last night one of them slap my girl in she face
The next time they see me, they better beware
I have an axe in my hand, a pistol in my waist,

---

*Trinidad expression meaning wildly outlandish.

When my gun shoot off the police could make their
    case. (p. 163)

His "I am the Ape Man not Tarzan" shows a maturity of humour that in
fact wins him the Calypso King Crown:

I am the ape man not Tarzan
This is something you have to understand
Tarzan couldn't be no ape
Anywhere in Africa he land we woulda cook him for
    dinner
He couldn't escape.

They just want to make me shame, giving Tarzan my
    fame
Imagine, this white man swinging from tree to tree
I must laugh at that, how could it be?
Is me! I am the monkey man, not he, (p. 230)

and this maturity of outlook is even the subject of an academic examination
by a University of the West Indies professor of English, who had already
turned his attention to Philo's first success. He wrote:

He has shown how ridiculous is the claim of the
western world, how overreaching and arrogant it has been
to suggest that an European lord would not only survive in
the jungle, but prevail as lord of all the African jungle, in
harmony with nature, a harmony that the European in
practice has long since subverted in favour of scientific
dissection, a practice that has increasingly alienated him
from himself.

Philo has in one blow put into perspective the utter
ridiculousness of the twin claims: the barbarity of the
blacks and the harmony with nature of the whites. (p. 231)

But though Philo clips the article for his scrapbook, "he wasn't sure he
understood the professor:"

The point he, Philo, was striving to make in the Tarzan
calypso was that the Africans would have eaten Tarzan if
he was real. He liked the idea of Africans as cannibals.
What a nice wicked sight! Tarzan in a big steaming iron
pot and Africans jumping around waiting for him to cook.
Any time he listened to that calypso he laughed. (p. 231)

One is immediately reminded of Sparrow's "Congo Man" which also dealt
with cannibalism (as a cover for other things, of course):

I envy the Congo Man
Ah wish ah coulda go and shake he han'
He eat until he stomach upset

And I...never eat a white meat yet

and of which Gordon Rohlehr has written:

> ...one couldn't play it to an African without some embar-
> rassment at the way in which the West Indian Negro can
> make the sort of joke about cannibalism of which only the
> white world ought to be capable. One couldn't play it to a
> European either except in a spirit of mockery which may
> itself be a comment on one's own insensitivity.[13]

It is perhaps for this reason among others that Victor Questel claimed that
"Philo's career sounds like Sparrow's."[14] Still, Philo reviews his past
records and realizes how much he was part of the calypso groove: "killing,
wounding, vilifying his childhood heroes, his friends, the bad Johns, the
Baptists, black women, his mother, his sisters, his self." But he realizes,
too, that he has moved away from all this: "Yes, he had moved on." (p.
233)

The final calypso on which we see Philo working is still unsung, but the
lyrics, our concern in this study anyway, show the calypsonian taking a
serious look at the sameness of the *nouveaux riches* in their well-appointed
suburban houses. Lovelace's build-up to the calypso is a telling comment on
the social levelling, indeed the horror, to use Philo's term, of middle class
external trappings:

> ...for the first time since coming here to live, he was
> struck by the newness and sameness of everything: the
> houses, lawns, motor cars in garages along whose walls the
> ivy sitting in their new ceramic pots had not yet begun to
> climb. (p. 213)

The calypso that springs to Philo's mind is no less equal to Lovelace's comment:

> The new people so new, you know, nobody
> Don't know who is who
> They so all the same, all of them carry
> The same kinda name
> Same kinda dog, same kinda wife, all of them living
> The same kinda life.
> . . .
> Cause the same kinda dress, same kinda shoe
> Same hair cut, same hair do
> I hear it is true, they all caress their wife
> On the same night too... (pp. 213-214)

Philo, then, becomes the folk philosopher and, once more, the social commentator. Whether or not he will return to the formula for success he had
found earlier is never known since he claims to be "going away." But it is
certain that if, or when, he continues to be "*role* serious, not real serious,"
according to Lovelace, he will be doing so with a renewed sense of his role

as calypsonian in the society, with the result that what comes over as not serious will in fact be deadly so.

The last example of the representation of the calypsonian as literary personage is taken from a source whose literary quality and aspiration some may still dispute, namely the comic strip. However, with the vast audience commanded by this popular form of "writing," it is evident that what their authors have to say cannot be disregarded as irrelevant to the society. The *Trinidad Express*, as well as its Sunday edition, carries a strip called "SweetBread," among whose characters—hen-pecked husband, domineering wife, school teacher, village drunkard, Chinese shopkeeper et al.—is calypsonian Kid Callalloo, faceless under his ever-present hat and forever strumming on his cuatro. Kid Callalloo, of the "Not So Young Brigade," is always promising to cop the main calypso honours but never manages anything more than off-colour puns and parodies of his fellow calypsonians. There is something of Ian McDonald's Jaffo in Kid Callalloo—not famous in the tents but always singing for his buddies. All in all, the creator of the strip seems aware of the problems facing the calypsonian in the society but never ventures into having Kid Callalloo compose, the way Lovelace's Philo does, any calypsoes that come under any of the generally recognized categories we have examined during the course of this study (except for humour, of course). Now this may not be feasible within the constraints of the four frames used during the week, but even with the added space of the Sunday full page, Kid Callalloo, who naturally appears more frequently during the calypso season, never comes up with anything resembling a full calypso stanza and chorus. Kid Callalloo therefore remains a figure of light comedy, in keeping, one might add, with the overall tone of the strip.

Such are the images of the calypso and the calypsonian in the literature of the country that has produced them. Though doubtlessly perpetuating stereotyped roles, some of these, as found in Earl Lovelace, for example, can go a long way toward demystifying the character that is the calypsonian, toward an understanding of the creative process involved in making a calypso, and, finally, toward giving the calypsonian increased literary and social respectability via the mesmerizing authority of the printed word on the Trinidad reading public as a whole.

Notes

[1] O.R. Dathorne (ed.), *Caribbean Verse* (London: Heinemann, 1967), p. 48.

[2] V.S. Naipaul, *Miguel Street* (Harmondsworth: Penguin Books, 1971), pp. 18-19. My emphasis. Subsequent references are to this edition.

[3] Kenneth Ramchand, *The West Indian Novel and its Background* (London: Faber and Faber, 1970), p. 102.

[4] Gordon Rohlehr, "The Folk in Caribbean Literature."

[5] Michel Fabre, "Moses and the Queen's English: Modified Dialect and Narrative Voice in Samuel Selvon's London Novels, "*Trinidad and Tobago Review,* Vol. 4, (Xmas 1980), p. 15.

[6] I am indebted to Rohlehr's article for these passages.

[7] Samuel Selvon, *A Brighter Sun* (London, Trinidad & Jamaica: Longman Caribbean, 1971), p. 86.

[8] Samuel Selvon, *The Lonely Londoners* (London, Trinidad & Jamaica: Longman Caribbean, 1972), pp. 111-112.

[9] Samuel Selvon, *Ways of Sunlight* (London, Trinidad & Jamaica: Longman Caribbean, 1973), p. 151. Subsequent references are to this edition.

[10] In Gabriel Coulthard (ed.), *Carribbean Narrative* (London: O.U.P.), 1966. SubwFquent references are to this edition.

[11] Earl Lovelace, *The Dragon Can't Dance* (London: André Deutsch, 1979), p. 112. Subsequent references are to this edition.

[12] Review in *Trinidad Guardian,* 29 January 1980.

[13] Gordon Rohlehr, "Sparrow and the Language of the Calypso," p. 95.

[14] Questel, loc. cit.

CONCLUSION

It is difficult to conclude a study of an art form that is still very much alive, and thus still evolving. Any definitive statements must necessarily refer to what has already happened, though the sobering perspective of time often also forces one to re-value original judgments. It is therefore less risky at this juncture to look at trends and budding developments to complement the descriptive and analytical examination we have made of the calypso over the past quarter of a century.

The form of the calypso has remained essentially the same—three or four stanzas plus chorus, with the inevitable innovations and variations introduced by individual styles. There has, however, been increased emphasis on the music accompanying the calypso, what with the enormous strides made in the field of electronics, allowing, for example, for 16 and 24-track recordings, precise mixing and an overall product that makes some of the earlier efforts on record sound as if they were recorded by mistake. This means that nearly every calypsonian is seeking to release a record of his work which, when done, sets a certain standard for the resident tent orchestra to try to achieve. It also means that the calypsonian works with a crowd of professionals—arrangers and the best studio musicians—and as a result has to acquire a professional approach as well. Gone are the days when the calypsonian simply asked the band for a key and sang his calypso, with the band striving earnestly to keep up.

One of the effects of this new emphasis on the music of the calypso is that the arrangers can work a mediocre lyric into a hit calypso via the music, played to the delight of dancers at parties and dances or on the radio stations. Also, in an unexpected return to the past, calypsoes have become longer, again to fit the demands of recording. Whereas the longer calypsoes had to be cut down to meet the constraint of the 78 r.p.m. record, the new 12-inch disco 45 has forced them to be lengthened again to fill out six or seven minutes. Unfortunately for the lovers of the calypso lyric (or for studies such as this one), the added material is nearly always the music, making the modern recordings a fertile ground for top-class arrangers, to whom many calypsonians owe more than passing credit for their success.

The contemporary calypsonian, then, sees himself more and more as professional entertainer in addition to being an artist, and it is in the combination of both these roles that lie his most serious problems. How long can he continue showing the commitment of the artist without the reward of the professional entertainer? It is clear that his role as "people's newspaper" is rather tenuous, since many other sources keep the Trinidad public abreast of whatever news or gossip that may interest it. As we have seen, weekly newspapers like *The Bomb* have virtually taken over this role; indeed, they probably provide the *sole* source of reading material for a substantial number of people eager to learn the latest "lowdown" on what is happening in and to the society. Though still the people's philosopher and interpreter of events, the calypsonian now has to tailor his calypso to suit this trend; social and political commentary has to be particularly witty or sarcastic if the calypsonian does not want to bore his listener who, in all likelihood, would have heard the lament or complaint in question several times already. Originality, therefore, becomes very crucial, and it is not surprising to find that in recent times many calypsonians have turned to the instant popularity and the relative safety of the yearly carnival-oriented calypso with its catchy tune and its easier demand lyric-wise: "We go wine/ This year seventy-nine"... "The fete mustn't done/ This year eighty-one"..., or of the old stand-by, the smutty calypso.

There continues to be controversy associated almost annually with some aspect of the calypso. Whereas the government authorities have refrained from openly censoring calypsoes considered potentially damaging to its political survival—though some calypsonians will still claim that they are victimized by the government's Carnival Development Committee, which decides who appears on what shows etc. during the Carnival season and, therefore, who shares in whatever money is available—various groups within the society continue to complain when they feel themselves vilified in calypso. In 1980, for example, the Spiritual Baptists, who have always had a rough time with the rest of the community as a whole, claimed that calypsonian Blue Boy mocked their religion in his "Soca Baptist" because what was sacred and spiritual to them was interpreted as mere "bacchanal" by the calypsonian, an opinion widely if unjustifiably held by many non-Baptists in Trinidad anyway. The Baptists were particularly offended by the fact that Blue Boy appeared on stage in a robe easily recognized as the type used by them, that he punctuated his stanzas with the ringing of a bell, a very significant symbol for them, and that he appeared to "catch the power" at the end of his performance. Where, then, does entertainment stop and vilification begin?

Hardly had the controversy with the Baptists been settled, that is if it ever really was, when the Hindu community objected to a line from Scrunter's "Take the Number," a calypso in which he advised all young girls to note the registration number of any strange car in which they accept a ride because "Hindu priest raping school children and all." The fact was that such an individual was *alleged* to have criminally assaulted a girl but up to the time of the calypso the allegation had not been proven. The calypsonian was guilty of nothing more than the prevalent Trinidad tendency to hold any accused as guilty, especially in the more sordid crimes. Indeed, many of those who have been subsequently cleared of charges have still found themselves ostracized due to the original allegation. In both instances, the Prime Minister, normally so aloof from and silent on issues of far greater significance in the society, speedily appealed for "good sense" to prevail and the radio stations, in their interpretation of his call, stopped airing the offending numbers or did so, in Scrunter's case, after the insertion of a new, less offending line. (Interestingly the revelers, in another show of popular justice, made "Soca Baptist" the run-away Road March.)

Calypsoes found objectionable are not new to the calypso world and indeed calypso and controversy seem to go hand in hand. The main point of contention, however, with the renewed scrutiny of calypso content brought about by each objection, is the right of the artist to comment freely on matters as he sees fit. Should he be censored, and if so, by whom? Can the society afford to muzzle its artists? Must the calypsonian be made, as was the case in the earlier days, to submit his lyrics for vetting prior to performance? In a tongue-in-cheek comment on this issue, one *Trinidad Express* journalist raised the spectre of the calypsonian having to submit his composition to the Caribbean Conference of Churches, thence to the Vatican and finally to the Trinidad Cabinet, which would probably take its own bureaucratic time before granting approval anyway! This type of situation will undoubtedly not arise, but the point is well taken. Where will it all end? What is to prevent any group from claiming that it has been wronged? Of course, let us not forget that others in the society *also* have rights, which no calypsonian should be allowed to infringe or disrespect, if only out of a sense of mutual respect. After all, calypsonians as a group are as aware as anyone else of exploitation and denigration in the society. How, then, does one reconcile both these rights in the interest of national unity and national culture? Clearly, tolerance will have to be exercised by one party and the other, and to a degree that is acceptable to both, for, as Scrunter himself reminds us in his "Take the Number," "is who in de kitchen does feel de heat."

There are encouraging signs that the society as a whole has begun to accord the calypso the prominence and respect so long demanded by the calypsonian. The Government Broadcasting Unit, for example, routinely illustrates its various programmes of information on government activities with appropriate selections from calypsoes, and several calypsonians are being invited to lecture on the art form to the schools, thus establishing quite early in the minds of the youth what the calypso is really about. In fact, the Mighty Chalkdust, himself a Secondary School teacher, has shown in his book *Carnival in Trinidad and Tobago* how the calypso can be used to help children develop sense impression, awareness and self expression. But "the road is long, with many a winding turn." The yearly complaint continues *ad nauseam:* no respect from those in authority (although they enjoy the calypso), no unity among the calypsonians, continued exploitation by tent managers and record producers, the too-seasonal nature of calypso etc. However, awareness of the problems is already a giant step toward solving them. The calypso, whatever form it may evolve into, is assured a future in Trinidad, one in which improvements are bound to occur, for, to end with a quotation from the effort that won 11-year-old Charmaine McCarthy the Junior Calypso Crown in 1979:

> Calypso is you, Calypso is me
> Calypso right here in T and T in everybody.

It is certain that the vibrancy of the calypso will not allow it to fade into oblivion, even though, as is the case with so many other societies world-wide, increased written literary output and rapid improvements in the technique of communication have taken their inevitable toll on the oral tradition of the people. The Trinidad society is, however, still small enough, still closely-knit enough, despite all its problems, for such a tradition to be appreciated and for an oral literature, the calypso in this instance, to exist alongside its written counterpart, thereby elevating the calypsonian, in the eyes of those who still need the re-assurance, to the rank of full-fledged literary artist.

APPENDIX
A QUARTER CENTURY
OF CHAMPIONS

Yr	Monarch[1]	Selections[2]	Road March	Calypsonian
56	Sparrow	Jean and Dinah	Jean and Dinah	Sparrow
57	Pretender	Que Sera, Sera	Drink Tisane de Durbon	N. Caton[3]
58	Striker	Don't Blame the P.N.M. Calypso Singing	Pay As You Earn	Sparrow
59	Striker	Ban the Hula Hoop West Indians in England	Run the Gunslingers	Caruso
60	Sparrow	Mae Mae Ten to One is Murder	Mae Mae	Sparrow
61	Dougla	Laziest Man Split Me in Two	Royal Jail	Sparrow
62	Sparrow	Sparrow Come Back Home Federation	Maria	Blakie
63	Sparrow	Dan is the Man Kennedy and Kruschev	The Road	Kitchener
64	Bomber	Bomber's Dream Joan and James	Mama, Dis is Mas	Kitchener
65	Sniper	Portrait of Trinidad More Production	My Pussin	Kitchener
66	Terror	Last Year's Happiness Steelband Jamboree	Obeah Wedding	Sparrow
67	Cypher	If the Priest Could Play Election Bacchanal	Sixty-seven	Kitchener
68	Duke	What is Calypso Social Bacchanal	Miss Tourist	Kitchener
69	Duke	Black is Beautiful Visina	Sa Sa Yay	Sparrow
70	Duke	Brotherhood of Man See Through	Margie	Kitchener
71	Duke	Mathematical Formula Melvie and Yvonne	Mas in Madison Square Garden	Kitchener
72	Sparrow	Rope Drunk and Disorderly	Drunk and Disorderly	Sparrow
73	Sparrow	Happy School Days Same Time, Same Place	Rainorama	Kitchener
74	Sparrow	We Pass That Stage Miss Mary	Bassman	Shadow

75	Kitchener[4]	Tribute to "Spree" Simon Fever	Tribute to "Spree" Simon	Kitchener
76	Chalkdust	Three Blind Mice Ah Put on Mih Guns Again	Flag Woman	Kitchener
77	Chalkdust	Juba Doo Bai Shango Vision	Tempo	Rose
78	Rose	I Thank Thee Her Majesty	Soca Jam	Rose
79	Stalin	Caribbean Man Play One	Ah Tell She	Poser
80	Relator	Food Prices Take a Rest	Soca Baptist	Blue Boy

[1]With the inclusion of female calypsonians, the Calypso King became the Calypso Monarch. Sobriquets are given less the "Mighty," "Lord," "Calypso" or "Black."

[2]From 1958 two calypsoes were judged for the competition.

[3]This was originally composed as an advertising jingle but caught the fancy of the revelers who supplied their own lyrics to the melody.

[4]From this year Kitchener and Sparrow publicly announced their withdrawal from the annual competition, but were still eligible for the Road March.

BIBLIOGRAPHY

[For the sake of convenience, titles which have appeared in the notes are repeated here, in the event that the notes were not consulted or that a particular chapter was not read.]

Abrahams, Roger. "The Shaping of Folklore Traditions in the British West Indies." *Journal of Inter-American Studies,* Vol. 9, No. 3 (July 1967), pp. 456-480. New York: Anchor Books, 1976, Chap. 7.

Adams, Alton. "Whence came the calypso." *Caribbean,* Vol. 8, No. 10 (1955), pp. 218-220, 230, 235.

Anthony, Michael. "Lord Beginner and the Old Calypso Days." *"Glimpses of Trinidad and Tobago.* Port of Spain: Columbus Publishing Company, 1974, pp. 58-64.

Anthony, Michael and Carr, Andrew, eds. *David Frost introduces Trinidad and Tobago.* London: A. Deutsch, 1975.

Attaway, William. *Calypso Song Book.* Ed. Lyle K. Engel. New York: McGraw-Hill, 1957.

Austin, R.L. "Understanding Calypso content: a critique and an alternative explanation." *Caribbean Quarterly,* Vol. XXII, Nos. 2 & 3 (June-September 1976), pp. 74-83.

Awonoor, Kofi. *The Breast of the Earth.* New York: Anchor Books, 1976.

Baugh, Edward, ed. *Critics on Caribbean Literature.* London: George Allen and Unwin, 1978.

Bennett, Louise. *Jamaica Labrish.* Jamaica: Sangster, 1966.

Blair, Dorothy. *African Literature in French.* Cambridge: Cambridge University Press, 1976.

Blake, Fedo. "Our Own Calypso: Its Birth, Revolution." *Sunday Guardian* (Trinidad), 29 January 1978.

Boyce, Carole E. "The Trinidad Calypso: An Analysis of the Functions of An African Oral Tradition in the Caribbean." M.A. Thesis, Howard University, 1974.

Brathwaite, Edward. "The African Presence in Caribbean Literature." *Daedalus,* Vol. 103, No. 2 (Spring 1974), pp. 73-109.

Brereton, Bridget. "The Trinidad Carnival, 1870-1900." *Savacou,* No. 11/12 (September 1975), pp. 46-57.

Brown, H. (Rap). *Die, Nigger, Die.* New York: Dial Press, 1969.

Brown, Lloyd. "Calypso Tradition in West Indian Literature." *Black Academy Review,* Vol. 2, Nos. 1 and 2, 1971, pp. 127-143.

Brown, Wenzell. *Angry Men, Laughing Men.* New York: Greenberg, 1947.

Caribbean Artists Movement. "Comments on Gordon Rohlehr's 'Sparrow and the Language of the Calypso.'" *Caribbean Quarterly,* Vol. XIV, Nos. 1 & 2 (March-June 1968), pp. 91-96.

Caribbean Quarterly, Vol. 4, Nos. 3 & 4 (March-June 1956). Special issue on Carnival.

Carr, Andrew. "The Calypso: A People's Poetic Platform." *West Indian World,* No. 215 (29 August-4 September 1975), pp. 12-13.

Carr, Andrew et al. *Independence Exhibition: History of Carnival, Calypso and Steelband.* Port of Spain: Trinidad Government Printery, 1962.

Constance, Zeno. "Blues and Rebellion. Poet and Prophet: A Look at Valentino." Caribbean Studies Thesis, University of the West Indies, St. Augustine, 1977.

Coombs, Orde, ed. *Is Massa Day Dead?* New York: Anchor Books, 1974.

Cooper, Rhonda. "Political Calypsoes from 1965 to 1975, with special reference to the Mighty Chalkdust." Caribbean Studies Thesis, University of the West Indies, St. Augustine, 1978.

Coulthard, Gabriel (ed.) *Caribbean Narrative.* London: Oxford University Press, 1966.

Crowley, D.J. "Toward a Definition of Calypso." *Ethnomusicology,* Vol. III, No. 2 (May 1959), pp. 57-66; Vol. III, No. 3 (September 1959), pp. 117-124.

————————. "Folk Etymology and Earliest Documented Usage of 'Calypso.'" *Ethnomusicology,* Vol. X, No. 1 (1966), pp. 81-82.

Cummins, W. *Calypsos, Symphonies and Incest.* Toronto: Arawak Publishing House, 1974.

Dathorne, O.R., ed. *Caribbean Verse.* London: Heinemann, 1967.

Deyal, Ena. "Black Stalin, Calypsonian: A Study." Caribbean Studies Thesis, University of the West Indies, St. Augustine, 1979.

Doyle-Marshall, William. "Calypso: The After-Season Scrunt." *People* (Trinidad), February-March 1978, pp. 58 & 61.

Duggan, Joseph. *Oral Literature: 7 Essays.* Edinborough & London: Scottish Academic Press, 1975.

Edwards, Bryan. *The History, Civil and Commercial, of the British Colonies in the West Indies.* Vol. II. London, 1819; rpt. New York: AMS Press, 1966.

Elder, J.D. "The Evolution of the Traditional Calypso of Trinidad and Tobago: A Socio-historical Analysis of Song-change." Ph.D. Thesis, University of Pennsylvania, 1966.

————————. "Social Development of the Traditional Calypso." University of the West Indies, St. Augustine, 1968.

————————. "The Male/Female Conflict in Calypso." *Caribbean Quarterly,* Vol. XIV, No. 3 (September 1968), pp. 23-41.

————————. *The Calypso and its Morphology.* Trinidad: National Cultural Council, 1973.

Espinet, C.S. and Pitts, H. *Land of the Calypso: The Origin and Development of Trinidad's Folksong.* Port of Spain, 1944.

Fabre, Michel. "Moses and the Queen's English." *Trinidad and Tobago*

Review, Vol. 4, No. 4 (Xmas 1980), pp. 12-13, 15.

Finnegan, Ruth. *Oral Literature in Africa.* London: Clarendon Press, 1970.

Hadel, Richard. "Black Caribbean folk music." *Caribbean Quarterly,* Vol. XXII, Nos. 2 and 3 (June and September 1976), pp. 84-96.

Hill, Errol. "Calypso." *Jamaica Journal,* Vol. 5, No. 1 (March 1971), pp. 23-27.

——————. "The Calypso." In *David Frost introduces Trinidad and Tobago,* pp. 73-83.

——————. "On the Origin of the Term Calypso." *Ethnomusicology,* Vol. XI, No. 3 (September 1967), pp. 359-367.

——————. *The Trinidad Carnival: Mandate for a National Theatre.* Austin: University of Texas Press, 1972.

Hodge, Merle. "The Shadow of the Whip: A Comment on Male-Female Relationships in the Caribbean." *Is Massa Day Dead?* pp. 111-118.

Hylton, Patrick. "The Politics of Caribbean Music." *The Black Scholar,* Vol. 7, No. 1 (September 1975), pp. 23-29.

Jahn, Janheinz. *Neo-African Literature: A History of Black Writing.* New York: Grove Press, 1968.

James, C.L.R. *The Future in the Present.* London: Allison and Busby, 1977. Chapter on the Mighty Sparrow.

James, Louis, ed. *The Islands in Between.* London: Oxford University Press, 1968.

Jourdain, Elodie. "Trinidad Calypso not Unique." *Caribbean Commission Monthly Information Bulletin,* Vol. 7, No. 10 (May 1954), pp. 221-222, 232.

La Fortune, Claudette. *Chalkie: Hollis Liverpool (The Mighty Chalkdust) and his Calypsoes.* Port of Spain, 1978.

Lamson, Sophie. "Music and Culture in the Caribbean." Master's Thesis, Wesleyan University, 1957.

Lekis, Lisa. "The Origin and Development of Ethnic Caribbean Dance and Music." Ph.D. Thesis, University of Florida, 1956.

Lewis, Linden. "The Mighty Shadow: On the Pointlessness of Human Existence." *Caribbean Review,* Vol. X, No. 4 (Fall 1981), pp. 20-33, 49-50.

Lewis, Roy. "Kaiso gone dread: Black Stalin, The Caribbean Man in Cultural Perspective." Unpublished Caribbean Studies Thesis, University of the West Indies, Trinidad, 1980.

Liverpool, Hollis. *Carnival in Trinidad and Tobago: Its Implications for Education in Secondary Schools.* Trinidad, 1979.

——————. "From the Horse's Mouth." Caribbean Studies Thesis, University of the West Indies, St. Augustine, 1973.

Lovelace, Earl. "The Beat, Sound and Soul of Calypso." *People* (Trinidad), January 1978. pp. 41-44.

——————. *The Dragon Can't Dance.* London: A. Deutsch, 1979.

Luis, Robert. *Authentic Calypso: the song, the music, the dance.* New York: Latin American Press, 1957.

Matthews, B. "Calypso and Pan-America." *Commonweal,* Vol. XXXVII (Nov. 13, 1942), pp. 91-93.

Mordell, Albert. *The Erotic Motive in Literature.* New York: Collier Books, 1962.

Naipaul, V.S. *The Middle Passage.* Harmondsworth: Penguin Books, 1969.

——————. *Miguel Street.* Harmondsworth: Penguin Books, 1971.

Niane, D.T. *Sundiata. An Epic of Old Mali.* London: Longmans, 1965.

Oxaal, Ivor. *Black Intellectuals Come to Power: The Rise of Creole Nationalism in Trinidad and Tobago.* Cambridge, Mass: Schenkman Publishing Company, 1968.

Payne, Gloria. "The Calypso in Grenada." *Grenada Independence 1974: Cultural Pot Pourri.* Grenada, 1974, p. 36.

Pearse, Andrew. "Carnival in Nineteenth Century Trinidad." *Caribbean Quarterly,* Vol. 4, Nos. 3 & 4 (March-June 1956), pp. 175-193.

Pearse, Andrew, ed. and arranger. "Mitto Sampson on Calypso Legends of the Nineteenth Century." *Caribbean Quarterly,* Vol. 4, Nos. 3 & 4 (March-June 1956), pp. 250-262.

Pitts, Harry. "Calypso: From Patois to its Present Form." *Sunday Guardian* (Trinidad and Tobago). Independence Supplement. August 26, 1962, pp. 41-43.

Quevedo, Raymond. "Executor and the Golden Age of Calypso Resurgence." *Sunday Guardian* (Trinidad), 9 February 1964.

——————. "History of Calypso, This Country of Ours." Independence Brochure. *The Nation* (Trinidad), 1962.

Ramchand, Kenneth. *The West Indian Novel and its Background.* London: Faber and Faber, 1970.

Ramcharan, Wendy. "Soca and its impact on the calypso." Unpublished Caribbean Studies Thesis, University of the West Indies, Trinidad, 1980.

Rennie, Bukka. "New Calypso Structure to suit the New Mood." *Kairi,* No. 2 (February 1974), pp. E.1.1-6.

Reyes, Elma. "What's in a Name? Quite a lot for the Calypsonians." *Trinidad Express,* 12 October 1979.

——————. "Women hold their own in Kaiso World." *Trinidad Express,* February 1979.

Roach, Glen. "Calypso and Politics, 1956-1972." Caribbean Studies Thesis, University of the West Indies, St. Augustine, 1972.

Roberts, J.S. *Black Music of Two Worlds.* London: Allen Lane, 1973. Chap. 5.

Rodman, Hyman. *Lower-class Families: The Culture of Poverty in Negro Trinidad.* New York: Oxford University Press, 1971.

Rohlehr, Gordon. "Calypso and Morality." *Moko,* 17 January 1969.
——————. "Calypso and Politics." *Moko,* 29 October 1971.
——————. "Calypso as Comment." *Listener,* February 1979, pp. 186-187.
——————. "The Folk in Caribbean Literature." *Tapia,* 17 December 1972.
——————. "Forty Years of Calypso." *Tapia,* Vol. 2, Nos. 1, 2 & 3, 1972.
——————. "Sparrow and the Language of the Calypso." *Savacou,* No. 2 (September 1970), pp. 87-99.
——————. "Sparrow as Poet." In *David Frost introduces Trinidad and Tobago,* pp. 84-89.
Russell, Helen. *West Indian Scenes.* London: Hale, 1942.
Ryan, Selwyn. *Race and Nationalism in Trinidad and Tobago.* Toronto: University of Toronto Press, 1972.
——————. "Voices of Protest." *Trinidad Carnival.* Trinidad: Key Caribbean, No. 7, 1979. n.pag.
Sander, Reinhard, ed. *From Trinidad: An Anthology of Early West Indian Writing.* London: Hodder and Stoughton, 1978.
Selvon, Samuel. *A Brighter Sun.* London, Trinidad & Jamaica: Longman, 1971.
——————. *The Lonely Londoners.* London, Trinidad & Jamaica: Longman, 1972.
——————. "Calypsonian." In Coulthard, G. (ed.). *Caribbean Narrative* London: O.U.P., 1966.
——————. *Ways of Sunlight.* London, Trinidad & Jamaica: Longman, 1973.
Sparrow, the Mighty (Slinger Francisco). *One Hundred and Twenty Calypsoes to Remember.* Port of Spain: National Recording Company, 1963.
Stollmeyer, Hugh. "The Calypso and Politics." *The Beacon,* Vol. 4, No. 1 (November 1939), pp. 13-14.
Warner, Keith Q. "Creole Languages and National Identity in the Caribbean." *CLA Journal,* Vol. XX, No. 3 (March 1977), pp. 319-332.
——————. "Léon Damas and the Calypso." *CLA Journal,* Vol. XIX, No. 3 (March 1976), pp. 374-381.
Wellek, René and Warren, Austin. *Theory of Literature.* Harmondsworth: Penguin Books, 1963.
Williams, Eric. *History of the People of Trinidad and Tobago.* Port of Spain: P.N.M. Publishing Company, 1962.
——————. *Inward Hunger.* London: A. Deutsch, 1969.
Van Dan, Theodore. "The Influence of the West African Songs of Derision on the New World." *African Music Society Journal,* Vol. I (1954).

SELECTED DISCOGRAPHY

Records listed hereunder are all 12-inch LP's and appear alphabetically under the main part of the calypsonians' sobriquet.

Belafonte, Harry. *Calypso Carnival.* RCA, LSP 4521.
—————. *Jump-up Calypso.* RCA, LSP 2388.
Christo, Lord. *Authentic Calypso with Lord Christo.* Mercury, MG 20297.
Chalkdust, Mighty. *Ah put on me guns again.* Strakers, GS 8886.
—————. *Teacher, Commoner and King.* Strakers, GS 8897.
—————. *The Mighty Chalkdust.* Strakers, GS 7784.
—————. *To Spree with Love.* Strakers, GS 7799.
—————. *Stay up.* Strakers, GS 7789.
Crazy, Calypso. *Crazy's Super Album.* Crazy Music, CM 001.
—————. *Madness is Gladness.* Crazy Music, CM 003.
Duke, Mighty. *Black is beautiful.* Tropico, TSI, 2017.
—————. *Calypso a la King.* Tropico, TSI, 2030.
—————. *Calypso—All Night Tonight.* Tropico, TLP 1000.
—————. *Cock of the Rock.* Star, SR 6666.
—————. *Exciting Calypso.* Tropico, TSI, 2023.
Explainer, Mighty. *Positive Vibrations.* Semp, SWH 001.
—————. *Something Special.* Boaex, Bax 001.
—————. *This is Explainer.* Umbala, UPLP 001.
Fighter, King et al. *Hellish Calypso.* Cook, 1122.
Francine, Singing et al. *Calypso in Rage.* Strakers, GS 7785.
Funny, Lord. *Have fun with Funny.* Antillana, ALPS 1014.
Jones, Patrick (Chinee Patrick). *Calypso Lore and Legend.* Cook, 5016.
Kitchener, Lord. *Carnival Fever.* Trinidad, TRCS 4000.
—————. *Curfew Time.* Trinidad, TRCS 0001.
—————. *Home for Carnival.* Kalinda, KDS 2006.
—————. *Hot and Sweet.* Trinidad, TRC 0005.
—————. *Hot Pants.* Trinidad, TRCS 0002.
—————. *Kitch '67.* RCA, LPB 3047.
—————. *Lord Kitchener's Greatest Calypso Hits.* RCA, LPS 3050.
—————. *Lord Kitchener sings Calypsos.* Songs of Caribbean, SLP 729.
—————. *Melodies of the 21st Century.* Trinidad, TRC 0006.
—————. *Play Mas with Kitch.* Tropico, TMI 2004.
—————. *Shooting with Kitch.* Trinidad, CR 140.
—————. *Sock it to me, Kitch.* Tropico, TSI 2018.
—————. *Spirit of Carnival.* Trinidad, TRCCS 007.
—————. *Tourist in Trinidad.* Trinidad, TRCS 003.
—————. *We walk 100 miles.* Trinidad, TRCS 003.

Layne, Lancelot. *Neo-Calypso*. Ka-La-Loo, KLS 051.

Lion, Roaring et al. *The Real Calypso, 1927-1946*. RBF 13.

Maestro, Lord. *Rampage*. Kalinda, KDS 2011.

Melody, Lord. *Again! Lord Melody sings Calypso*. Cook, 914.

_____. *I Man*. EddyMel, 001.

_____. *Lord Melody: Calypso 1962*. Cook, 931.

_____. *Sugar Jam*. EddyMel, 002.

_____. *Through the Looking Glass*. Cook, 927.

Melody, Lord et al. *Top Calypsonians*. RCA, LPB 3018.

Rose, Calypso. *Her Majesty*. CLO 444.

_____. *Mass Fever*. CLO 666.

_____. *We rocking for Carnival*. CLO, CR 251.

Shadow, Mighty. *Bass Man*. Strakers, GS 7792.

_____. *De Zess Man*. Shadow, CR 143.

_____. *Doh mess wid meh head*. Kalinda, KDS 2021.

_____. *Dreadness*. RMP 1006.

_____. *If I coulda, I woulda, I shoulda*. Kalinda, CR 153.

_____. *The flip side of Shadow*. RMP 1006.

Shorty, Lord. *Endless Vibrations*. Shorty, SLP 1004.

_____. *Soca Explosion*. Charlie's, SCR 1004.

_____. *Sokah: Soul of Calypso*. Semp.

_____. *Sweet Music*. Shorty, SLP 1003.

Sniper, Mighty. *Calypso*. National, NLP 4141.

Sparrow, Mighty. *Angostura congratulates the Mighty Sparrow*. JAF 001.

_____. *Birdie: The Calypso Genius*. National, NLP 8420.

_____. *Boogie Beat*. Semp, SSL 016.

_____. *Calypso a la King*. Hilary, RALP 2122.

_____. *Calypso Carnival*. RA 2127.

_____. *Calypso Maestro*. RA 5050.

_____. *Calypso Sparrow*. RCA, LPS 3010.

_____. *Calypso Time*. Hilary, RA 2121.

_____. *Hotter than ever*. RA 3112.

_____. *King Sparrow's Calypso Carnival*. Cook, LP 920.

_____. *Knock dem down, Sparrow, knock dem down*. RA 4020.

_____. *Many moods of Sparrow*. Strakers, BW 1001 B.

_____. *More Sparrow More*. RA 2020.

_____. *More Sparrow's Greatest Hits*. RCA, LPB 1086; Tropico, 1086.

_____. *New York City Blackout*. Charlie's, CR 139.

_____. *Pussy Cat Party*. Sparrow's Hide-away, SH 2237.

_____. *Slave*. National, NLP 4188; Hilary, SP 3003.

_____. *Sparrow*. RCA, LPB 9035.

_____. *Sparrow at the Hilton*. RA 8070.

_____. *Sparrow at the Sheraton*. RA.

——— ———. *Sparrow: Calypso King*. RCA, LPB 1097.

——————— ———. *Sparrow's Carnival 1965*. National, 5050 A.

——————— ——. *Sparrow Come Back*. RCA, LPS 3006; Tropico 3006.

——————— ——. *Sparrow Dragon*. SpaLee 001.

———————. *Sparrow in Hi-Fi*. Cook 1126.

———————. *Sparrow in London*. RA 2127.

——————— ——. *Sparrow meets the Dragon*. SpaLee 001.

———————. *Sparrow Power*. RA 3030.

———————. *Sparrow Spectacular*. WIRL, W 034; Bestway, W 034.

———————. *Sparrow the Conqueror*. RCA, LPB 2035.

——————— . *Sparrow vs the Rest*. Tysott, SP 1976.

———————. *Spicy Sparrow*. RA 1005 S.

———————. *Tattoo Woman*. Hilary, SP 3002.

———————. *The Mighty Sparrow*. RCA, LPB 1056.

———————. *The Outcast*. National, NLP 4199.

———————. *This is Sparrow*. Balisier, HDF 1008.

Sparrow, Mighty et al. *Calypso Kings and Pink Gin*. Cook 1185.

Spoiler, Mighty. *The Immortal Spoiler*. RA 4040.

Stalin, Black. *The Caribbean Man*. Wizards.

Superior, Brother. *A New Beginning*. Mabel.

Terror, Mighty. *Best of golden voice Terror*.

Tiger, Growling. *High Priest of Mi Minor*. Rounder 5006.

Valentino, Brother. *Third World Messenger*. Semp 5012.